Despite This Flesh

DESPITE THIS FLESH

The Disabled in Stories and Poems

Edited by Vassar Miller

UNIVERSITY OF TEXAS PRESS, AUSTIN

Copyright © 1985 by the University of Texas Press
All rights reserved
Printed in the United States of America

First Edition, 1985

Requests for permission to reproduce material from this work should be sent to
Permissions, University of Texas Press, Box 7819, Austin, Texas 78713.

Library of Congress Cataloging in Publication Data
Main entry under title:

Despite this flesh.

1. Physically handicapped—Literary collections.
2. American literature—20th century.   3. English
literature—20th century.   I. Miller, Vassar.
PS509.P58D48   1985   810'.8.'03520816   85-632
ISBN 0-292-72449-7
ISBN 0-292-71550-1 (pbk.)

Dedicated to Meeme,
a child with cerebral palsy
supported through the Christian Children's Fund

Contents

Acknowledgments

I wish to thank Dr. David Bybee for reading the selections of my anthology; Edward Osaski and the main branch of the Houston Public Library for locating various poems and stories about the disabled; Jackie Simon and her class in the Houston Community College for helping me with the word count in my manuscript; and Helen Williams for serving for a time as assistant editor. I also wish to thank my secretaries, Penelope Loughhead and Carol Anglin, and my housekeeper, Rosalie Grace, for their patience in helping me.

Introduction

"Attention must be paid to this man!" cries Willy Loman's widow in *The Death of a Salesman*. Just so, this anthology was born from the conviction that attention must be paid to one of the world's most invisible minorities, the physically handicapped. The attention does not denigrate the attention paid by dedicated consumer advocates and legislators. Neither, of course, does it extol the dubious attention rendered by the gawking of an overcurious and underinformed public. This assertion does, however, call for that alert attention demanded by any human being made in the image of God, or at least according to the philosophical notion that every human being is a human being, no less and no more. The handicapped have, to a large extent, come out of the back bedroom, to which an ignorant past has relegated them. The purpose of this anthology is to ensure also that the disabled come out of the back bedroom of the mind and so liberate not only the captives but also the captors. For any jail, however benign, imprisons jailor as well as jailed.

Furthermore, this assertion does not deny the transcendently alert attention already paid to the disabled in the past. I think of Christy Brown, cerebral palsied author of *Down All the Days* and other books, and his devoted mother. Victim of a drunken husband and mother of twenty-two children, she took time to notice five-year-old Christy playing with a piece of chalk held between his toes and taught him to read and write. I think of my own young stepmother, writing out for me on a lined tablet the sentences she recalled from her own primer, "This is May. This is Will. How do you do, May? How do you do, Will?" The following year she went to the school office and obtained books proper to my age and grade level. For I grew up in the time before either special education or mainstreaming. She had tried to enroll me in a private school. "They just looked at me and started talking about God!" she said in dismayed tones. She, and later my father, undertook my education until I was twelve and started to public school.

The sad truth remains, though, that despite past exceptions and present progress, reality forever lags behind the dream. The handicapped (like everyone else, true, but right now I'm talking about the *physically* handicapped) too often have been and are being killed by kindness, stifled by overprotection, choked by subtle if sometimes unconscious snubs by genuinely good people who would swear to preferring death over hurting anybody. Such treatment, most often misguided rather than intentional, can lead to what Elizabeth Bowen called "the death of the heart." Perhaps the saddest truth, however, is that some of this slow death is self-inflicted; too many handicapped folk linger, bound by anger, depression, self-pity, or fear in the back bedrooms of their own minds. It is to prevent such pointless dying that this anthology has come into being.

One more anthology in a market already glutted by anthologies dealing with minorities and nearly every other subject you can name is, even so, desirable and helpful. Desirable, because, as editor of *Despite This Flesh*, I have done my best to include in it only material of high literary excellence. Helpful, because if the general public is uninformed it needs to be exposed, and what better means of exposure than good literature?

This anthology is also intended to assist public schoolteachers now engaged in what frequently must be the baffling task of mainstreaming handicapped students. True, one of my correspondents has written me pessimistically, "We may all question the extent to which 'teachers' can be enlightened. The principal motivation toward their career is that which a kindly heart may bring to their relationship. Otherwise it's a salaried job. . . . Comprehension can be neither added nor subtracted." My sole measure of the accuracy of my correspondent's remarks comes from what I remember about some of my teachers. My high school history teacher, for instance. Whenever I found a teacher with patience for my halting speech, I liked to indulge in reciting. Miss Covington let me, but even she had limits. "Just tell us in one word, Vassar," she would say. Miss Covington and I have remained fast friends. Being of conservative bent, she has occasionally grumbled about educational jargon come into fashion since her teaching days: "I didn't teach children," she insists. "I taught history *to* children. Emphasis on the preposition!" Sorry, Miss Covington. You're wrong. You taught me! May this anthology be a friend to good teachers like you in mainstreaming the handicapped, now that there is a name for what you did. Because mainstreaming the handicapped into school and into life is an essential goal in the just social order toward which teachers can work together sometimes more effectively than lobbyist and legislator. More important, this anthology may help disabled persons toward a better self-image, toward the certainty that if society sometimes peddles a "bill of goods" the disabled need not buy it.

Some such inspiration struck when one April afternoon I sat reading Anne Tyler's short story, "Average Waves in Unprotected Waters," about a mother forced to institutionalize her retarded son. I was also naturally curious about how writers view the handicapped. So, I sent out letters to poets and fiction writers, asking not only for original manuscripts but also for suggestions as to where to find other material. The response was overwhelmingly generous. I placed notices in *Coda*, publication of Poets & Writers, and notice led to notice even without my knowledge. I combed the library for authors past and present. In short, I had my curiosity satisfied.

In the process I made some fascinating discoveries, not the least of which is the difficulty of defining the term "handicap." I received many stories about the emotionally and mentally disturbed. Well, God knows, not to mention persons so afflicted, that psychiatric illness is a handicap. But such illness, it seemed to me, deserved an entire anthology to itself. I received submissions about cancer patients and people with other physical maladies. That such sicknesses handicap, even kill, no one can deny. But again, I thought, that isn't precisely what I want. A well-known poet wrote me that time is the real handicap. True enough—nobody can make bargains with death. Another wrote that we are all handicapped and some of us know it. Again true, but saying that is rather like telling the patients in the terminal ward that everyone is terminal. An anthology based on this definition would include every good piece of writing in history! A doctor of mine finally offered the suggestion that what I was really looking for was material about persons with motor and sensory dysfunctions. This definition, while not very literary, at least has the virtue of including not only the blind, the deaf, and the crippled but the retarded and the dyslexic as well, since their malfunctions are rooted in and result in motor and sensory difficulties.

My own definition, I suppose, is that a physical handicap is whatever physical defect sets people to staring or whispering when a person goes down the street. My own personal observation has been that what handicaps me far more than my physical condition of cerebral palsy is the reaction society has to it and, no less important, my reaction to society's reaction. In the final analysis, any definition is mutually agreed upon.

Another discovery I made, sometimes disappointing, sometimes delightful, is the extent to which writers share the views of their culture regarding the disabled. The writer's eye is supposed to spy out what no other eye can, and the poet's eye is supposed to be particularly free of prejudice. Yet sometimes they hold up the mirror, not to nature but to society. Of course, they can do it, fully aware that the mirrored image is warped. Sometimes they seem not to be thus aware. Occasionally it is difficult to tell when they are and when they are not. Are the anti-Semitic elements present in *The Merchant of Venice* there despite Shakespeare's knowledge that anti-Semitism is vicious nonsense, or is Shakespeare simply genius enough, despite his own anti-Semitism, to humanize Shylock? Nevertheless, tongue-in-cheek or not, this mirrored image presents the Jew as evil. So such an image displays the idiot as pathetic, the blind man sad, the cripple grotesque. The writer, whether concurringly or pejoratively, reflects the world's opinion: the race is to the swift and the battle to the strong.

Perhaps the writer assumes the ancient superstitions: the disabled is magic or superlatively gifted by God. I have often been told, "If you weren't handicapped you probably wouldn't write poetry." What about the myriad other poets who have no visible handicap? The afflicted one is the bait dropped in the waters of chaos to catch whatever fish of meaning may surface to take it and so let normal humanity know that, after all, everything is well. People usually feel guilty in the presence of the handicapped. Even the moderately disabled may feel guilty before the severely disabled. But if the maimed person is that way for a reason, set apart, "special," to use the current silly euphemism, then the rest of humanity can rest comfortably. The blind man, being always wise, should feel favored. The crippled girl, being perpetually sweet, should regard herself blessed. The cliché sings out the hours of darkness while we all sleep snugly.

Or the writer can reverse the situation. Magic can be black. The hunchback is evil, the blind man conniving, and the cripple lecherous. Furthermore, the writer can indulge in cheap shots at the expense of a malignant or an uncaring God or even one who has the nerve not to exist, can back the universe into a corner and snarl, "You Bastard, look what You've done!" In short, the handicapped provide fine bait for the fishers of stereotypes and not of reality.

When all is said and done, however, the stereotype of a literary genius is preferable to that of a philistine. Better Dickens' sentimental portrayal of Tiny Tim perched winsomely upon his father's shoulder than the portrayal of me implied by a Sunday School teacher chirping over me years ago, "Bless her heart! I bet she knows every hymn in the hymnbook," merely because I had told her the page number of "Onward Christian Soldiers." Or a woman's stereotyping of a friend of mine when, seeing him seated in his wheelchair in his van, she exclaimed, "Isn't that sweet! He's reading his Bible." Charles was perusing the *Wall Street Journal*.

Moreover, a great writer cannot present a straight stereotype. He or she makes it slightly cattywumpus. The Shylock of Shakespeare is a real human being, whereas the Jew of Malta as portrayed by Marlowe, also a master but a lesser one, is a farcical villain. Likewise, Shakespeare humanizes the wicked Richard III. No reasonably sane person would touch Richard's hump for luck (unless to do it and run), but in his famous monologue we can only sympathize when he growls:

> I, that am not made for sportive tricks.
> Nor made to court an amorous looking glass;
> I, that am rudely stamped and want love's majesty
> To strut before a wanton ambling nymph;
> I, that am curtail'd of this fair proportion,
> Cheated of feature by dissembling nature,

> Deform'd, unfinish'd, sent before my time
> Into this breathing world, scarce half made up,

until, as he continues, "And that so lamely and unfashionable / That dogs bark at me as I halt by them; . . . / And therefore, since I cannot prove a lover / To entertain these fair-well-spoken days, / I am determined to prove a villain," we are half-tempted to wish him luck.

Flannery O'Connor performs variations on yet another stereotype of the disabled, that of the embittered cripple. So unsentimental, she occasionally makes her most ardent admirer weep for saccharin. She depicts the Bible salesman stealing the thoroughly unpleasant Hulga's leg. But O'Connor knows perfectly well that Hulga is embittered less because of her wooden leg than because Hulga's mother "thought of her as a child though she was thirty-two years old and highly educated." Also the tedious diet of platitudes served up by her mother would make a sourpuss of the sunniest saint. Certainly if Shakespeare twists one stereotype, O'Connor tosses another to hell. Shakespeare skews the Elizabethan concept of a deformity, malignant and opposed to nature, just enough to illuminate the fact that the literary master of masters sees true in spite of himself. O'Connor has the self-avowed and valid ambition of writing in large letters to make the blind see. Shakespeare sets himself the more difficult and delicate task of making the sighted look squarely at what is right before them.

The best way for a writer to deal with any stereotype is neither to bend it nor to blast it, but to ignore it as Ernest Herbert does in his novel, *The Dogs of March*. The protagonist, Howard Elman,

> would not admit to himself that he was getting hard of hearing, and as a result he yelled all the time, even when he thought he was speaking softly. Furthermore, he set strangers against him by another habit growing out of his poor hearing. He had a coarse, pitted face, and his practice of shaving at night, instead of in the morning, gave him a perpetually unkempt look. When he stared, his mouth twisted into a grimace, and his gray bullet eyes seemed to shoot into others' most private thoughts, when in fact he was using his eyes to help him hear.

But Howard's growing deafness isn't the thing that bothers him. What worries him the most, what, in fact, enrages him, is his near illiteracy. Add to this trouble his problems with family, his difficulty with neighbors, his bouts with brute circumstance and you have one more crazy quilt of the human condition.

Christy Brown in *Down All the Days* gently destroys yet another hackneyed image of the disabled person as an asexual creature by showing the brothers of the protagonist, who is severely crippled with cerebral palsy, pulling him along in a wagon to a naughty peep show:

> Some of the boys were very quiet, very intent, absorbed in watching; others whistled, and howled, and slapped their thighs or the behinds of their mates, and cries of "Will yous look at that!" and "Look at the dollies on that wan!" Presently his big brother came back, rubbing his eyes with his knuckles, and looked down at him thoughtfully, then grinned and pushed him in the boxcar up to one of the machines.
>
> "Jesus, no!" cried his eldest brother Jem, rushing over in panic when he divined Tony's lewd intention, his honest fat face showing real horror. "You can't show them dirty pictures to a cripple!" The others all laughed; Tony gave Jem a shove that sent him sprawling, then hoisted his crippled brother onto his shoulder. From his perch on that broad promontory, he could see inside the "picture box" quite clearly, and he was amazed at what he saw.

As would any other callow boy.

And the wife of the paralyzed man in the powerfully erotic poem "Seated Nude" by Richard Ronan, far from feeling him a pale creature too pure or too inept for sex, finds him an eminently satisfying lover. All such samplings from literature suggest that what the handicapped man or woman does on his or her "day off," to paraphrase Joseph Collin Murphey's whimsical title for his whimsical poem,* is to be a human being.

May *Despite This Flesh* serve as midwife to this kind of humane and clear-sighted understanding.

Vassar Miller

---

* "What the Paralytic Is Doing on His Day Off."

Despite This Flesh

Let us not always say,
"Spite of this flesh today
I strove, made head,
    gained ground upon the whole"
As the bird wings and sings,
Let us cry, "All good
    things are ours,
    nor soul helps flesh
    more, now, than
    flesh helps soul!"

—Robert Browning, "Rabbi Ben Ezra"

Yoke in His Youth

These selections deal with the grief, guilt, shame, and resentment imposed by disability on the young and their families. The troubles of the young always seem more poignant. Fathers reflect on the deafness of their children in poems by Robert Pawlowski and James Wright. Cheri Fein in "My Family Is Unhappy" shows one sister resentful of the attention given her crippled sister, who in turn resents her normal sister's ability to walk. Yet the unhappiness started before the disabling accident. In Anne Finger's story "Like the Hully-Gully but Not So Slow," the braces of the girl who is the protagonist scarcely figure. But they are a source of curiosity and the butt of her sister's annoyance. Yet the crippled girl knows that the braces are not her real problem, much less her main interest. She will wear her yoke with a difference.

At the School for the Deaf

Here
His gentle speech
Opens and draws closer,
And the raw, cupped
Hands he holds take place, like stones,
To address the air empty seas live inside,
Trapped, as they are, around curled shells: slowly,
He rocks the wind through sounds
The echoes themselves
Do not hear until
The fingered order
Works
And the stones
Open shells
To the air where I can hear
My deaf, my gentle
Son
Name each sea.

Reprinted from the *Carleton Miscellany*, copyright © by Carleton College, October 5, 1966.

Mutterings over the Crib of a Deaf Child

"How will he hear the bell at school
Arrange the broken afternoon,
And know to run across the cool
Grasses where the starlings cry,
Or understand the day is gone?"

Well, someone lifting curious brows
Will take the measure of the clock.
And he will see the birchen boughs
Outside sagging dark from the sky,
And the shade crawling upon the rock.

"And how will he know to rise at morning?
His mother has other sons to waken,
She has the stove she must build to burning
Before the coals of the nighttime die;
And he never stirs when he is shaken."

I take it the air affects the skin,
And you remember, when you were young,
Sometimes you could feel the dawn begin,
And the fire would call you, by and by,
Out of the bed and bring you along.

"Well, good enough. To serve his needs
All kinds of arrangements can be made.
But what will you do if his finger bleeds?
Or a bobwhite whistles invisibly
And flutes like an angel off in the shade?"

He will learn pain. And, as for the bird,
It is always darkening when that comes out.
I will putter as though I had not heard,
And lift him into my arms and sing
Whether he hears my song or not.

Like the Hully-Gully but Not So Slow

They have this rule here at the library that we innocent young things under the age of sixteen aren't allowed in the Adult Room. I guess they're afraid we'll pick up a copy of *Lolita* or *The Carpetbaggers* and see something raunchy and our minds will be permanently warped. So if you want to read something besides *Sue Barton at Nursing School*, *Beanie Goes to College*, or *The Wonderful World of Electricity*—the books that they have in the Young Adult section—then you've got to fill out this Book Request Slip for the librarian and she goes and fetches whatever it is you want. That way, there's no chance that your eyes will alight on anything forbidden.

I pass my slip to the librarian.

"Aren't you old enough to————"

"I'm eleven."

"Eleven?" she asks. She gives me a cool long once-over, down and then up, with her gaze finally coming to rest on my breasts.

I hunch my shoulders, suck in my chest. "Eleven," I say, in a disgusted tone of voice, to show her that I don't like it one bit better than she does. People are always acting like it's my *fault*, for Christ's sake. "Precocious puberty," that's what the doctor said. "Nothing to be alarmed about." Easy for him to say: he wasn't five feet tall at the age of eight; sprouting breasts and hair in strange places. Bleeding. "Too bad you're not a dairy cow." That's what my father said. "You'd be worth something then." He's a stupid bastard, which is not just my individual opinion. It happens to be a fact. F-A-C-T. Ask anyone.

The librarian returns with her arms full of books. "Do you really think you're going to be able to understand these?"

I shove my library card across the counter; give her one of my well-practiced glares.

She offers me a smile as a peace token, asks: "How did you break your leg?"

I lean slightly across the counter. "I was born this way," I hiss.

My parents' house is really pretty classy. It's this big old Victorian job, three stories, twelve rooms. The only reason we can afford it is that it's on the wrong side of Hope Street—*i.e.*, too close to where the Negroes live. I mean, I really can't believe that grown adults would not want to buy a house because Negroes live two blocks away, but that's the way the world is. I'm not complaining. We've got this nice house because of it.

Guess I'm the first one home: the mail is still lying on the floor under the mail slot. I dump my bookbag and crutches in the corner of the hall, go back and pick it up. There's a letter from some guy named Dr. Fishbien—I don't know who the hell he is, just that my father's always getting bills from him. Yesterday's *New York Times*, *The Proceedings of the American Academy of Philology*—my parents' dull stuff. They have such boring lives—sometimes I don't know how they manage to stay awake through them.

I go up the backstairs, which were made for the servants to use. My mother's old green bookbag from college is slung over my shoulder: it slops from side to side, banging against my crutches as I climb the stairs. My room's on the third floor, in the front of the house. It's kind of a lookout—I can keep an eye on who's coming and going. Usually, I'm looking out the window around six o'clock when my father comes home from work. I try to figure out from the way he pulls his VW into the driveway what kind of a mood he's in. Sometimes he's furious, racing headlong for the end of the drive and you think he's not going to stop, just keep going, smash into the chain link fence that separates our property from the Patinskys' and keep hurtling on—and then, at the last second, he slams on the brakes and the car lurches to a halt. Other days, it's a sad, slow creep.

God, I hate these braces. I have to get up fifteen minutes earlier than everybody else and start strapping and buckling myself into them. I'm supposed to leave them on until I go to bed at night, but forget it.

I sit down at my desk; stack my library books next to me. People are always asking me: "What kind of a scientist are you going to be?" I shrug my shoulders and say, "I don't know." But the truth of it is that I don't want to limit myself to just one thing—I want to know everything there is to know. Everything about physics, everything about astronomy, zoology, electrical engineering, chemistry—organic and inorganic—microbiology. Everything.

Even when I can't understand all the books I read, I love the sounds of the words: quantum, lambda, muon, strangeness is not conserved, klystron, well-collimated beam.

"Do you believe it?"

"I would never . . ."

"I'd just want to *di-ie* if . . ."

Giggle, giggle, giggle. That's my sister Suzanne and her best friend, Doreen. That's D as in dopey, O as in obnoxious, R as in rancid, E as in— never mind.

Suzanne is my older sister. She's fourteen. Frankly, I've known two-year-olds who were more mature. She and Doreen are probably going to spend the afternoon practicing their giggles. Or maybe they'll discuss eyebrow plucking. Talk about whether they'd rather have an XKE or a

Sting Ray. Did you hear about the new French teacher? I think Howie Abbot's a creep.

"Listen," Suzanne is saying as they go into her bedroom and shut the door. "Did you know she made out with . . ."

"Euuuuhhh," Doreen says. "Gross me out."

"Turn up the radio a little bit, would you? I don't want my stupid *sister*," she's practically shouting, "EAVESDROPPING."

Doreen starts fiddling with the radio dial, "Coming at you live from Providence, Rhode . . . ," a bleep of sound, another bleep, "WJ . . . *kind of like the monkey, kind of like the fish . . .*"

"I love this song."

"*Pretend you're in the water and*—I was just so pissed off at her, she's such an—*like the hully-gully but not so slow . . .*"

My door yanks open: "Would you fucking stop listening?"

"I'm not—"

"Sure. You're just sitting there. With your ear practically to the wall."

"I'm *thinking*."

"What are you *thinking* about?"

"The human condition," I say.

"The human condition," Suzanne snorts. "God. You're such an asshole. I wish you weren't my sister. I was sitting in algebra class during fourth period and you walked down the hall. Everyone heard you. Clunk. Squeak. Clunk. Squeak. Why don't you ever oil yourself?" And she slams the door shut.

Screw you. Just for that, I'm not ever going to oil them again. I'm going to let them get so bad that the whole school will be able to hear me coming when I walk down the empty hallways; I'll creak and the walls will echo back, "Creak: CREAK."

I pull my notebook out from under my pillow, cross off "1758"; next to it I write, "1757." Only one thousand seven hundred and fifty-seven days of this crap left. Then I will be sixteen years old. Sixteen. I will walk into the principal's office and say: "Mr. Dolan. I am withdrawing from school." "Excuse me?" He'll think he heard wrong. "Today's my sixteenth birthday. I am withdrawing from school. Quitting."

Then, I'll go to Paris—free myself from the straitjacket of this provincial town. Like Madame Curie, I'll go to the Sorbonne, starve in an attic, live on black bread and tea. I will waste. I suck in my cheeks, anchoring them between my teeth, to get an idea of how I will feel when my dedication to science has burned away all but my flesh. I have $143— babysitting money—saved up now. At the current rate of exchange, that is 623 French francs.

"Dinner!" my mother hollers up the stairs. "Re-bec-ca! Su-zanne! Ka-ate! Jim-my! Din-ner!"

Our dining-room furniture is old, made of mahogany, hand-carved. My parents got it second-hand from this crackpot professor ermitus, or however the hell you pronounce it, who was about to be carted off to a nursing home for doddering intellectuals.

My father sits at the head of the table in a chair with arms that are carved into great curlicues, ending in the heads of animals—dogs, maybe; or lions—with teeth bared. My mother sits at the foot of the table. Her chair has arms too, but plain ones.

I sit between my mother and Rebecca. A place of great safety: flanked on my left side by my mother's gentleness, on the right by Rebecca's coldness.

My father stands, the carving knife in one hand, the sharpening steel in the other. With a long clean motion he slices the knife against the sharpener. We are all studying his face, watching for a sign of his mood.

He sets a slice of beef on the first plate, passes it to Rebecca, who passes it to me. I hand it to my mother. She dollops instant mashed potatoes and canned peas onto it and returns it to me.

"Well," my mother says when we have all been served; we bend over our plates. But my father is sitting, hands folded in front of him on the table, not eating.

"Josh?" my mother ventures.

"I taught the most fascinating class today. Sometimes I think, gee whiz, Josh, you sure are a boring old windbag. Do you ever have those days? When you look out at your students and they're sitting there with chins resting in their hands, two kids in the back row are playing footsie, and you think, 'What the hell am I doing here?' You ever have those days?"

"Sometimes," my mother says hesitantly.

He stands up. "Today," he says, holding his open hands, slightly cupped, in front of him, "today I taught the most marvelous class." He brings his fingers to this thumbs, a gesture of appreciation. "Different theories on the nature and creation of the universe. This is fascinating," he says, and we obediently all set our knives and forks down on our plates and turn our heads toward him. He is leaning across the table now, hands clutching the edge, eyes glistening. "There are two main theories, Steady State and Big Bang. Steady State posits that the universe has always existed in its present form and always will. Big Bang says that the universe was created about eighteen billion years ago . . . primordial fireball. . . . of course, the universe is expanding . . ."

He sketches out our possible futures: a steady universe in which the stars and galaxies drift slowly apart, growing colder and colder, floating away from each other into the nothingness of space. I don't like that idea much. Or a universe expanding until like a rubber band it snaps back, atoms imploding, worlds destroyed.

"Some say the world will end in fire," my mother quotes, "some say——"

The telephone rings.

And rings again. Each burr lashes across the room like lightning.

"I don't want to hear that goddamn telephone," he shouts.

Suzanne pushes back her chair and dashes for it. "Fine," she whispers. "Listen, I can't talk to you now. You know. My father."

I squish my peas into my mashed potatoes with my fork. The green oozes into the white: squish; squish. I sneak a glance at my father. His eyes are on Suzanne, cold and fierce.

"Hang that goddamn thing up!" he shouts.

"There he goes," Suzanne whispers.

"Hang it up!" His hands are shaking. "Sit down." His upper lip is pointed, like the beak of a hawk.

"I don't want to hear that telephone ring one more time tonight."

"Mommy," Suzanne pleads as she takes her seat.

"Shut up," he says.

In the back of the *New York Times Magazine* every Sunday there's an advertisement that says, "Your Thoughts Have Wings." Underneath, there is a drawing of a man with a mystical look on his face and winged orbs flying from his head: his thoughts with wings. Underneath it explains how, through studious concentration, you can beam your thoughts into the minds of others. (There's a coupon underneath which you can mail to the Rosicrucians, who will send you more information. But of course, I don't dare . . . suppose I didn't get to the mail first.)

I am sending a thought throughout the city of Providence: "Don't call Suzanne tonight. Don't call her. She'll get in trouble with her father. Don't call." I send my winged orb flying down Lancaster Street; it makes a left turn onto Hope Street, floats up Doyle Avenue, slowly oozing its way out over the whole East Side: a fog of "Don't call. Don't call Suzanne Evans. Don't call."

I don't have to worry about the phone ringing and it being for me— the last time anybody called me was three weeks ago. It was Charlotte Rodriquez, who sits next to me in homeroom. She said, "We just got a telephone. I'm calling everybody I know."

"Oh," I said.

"So how are you doing?"

"Pretty good," I said. I moved my jaw up and down as if I were chewing a piece of gum. These were the things I was supposed to do: chew gum, talk on the telephone. "Pretty good," I said again.

"Yeah?"

"Yeah. How about you?"

"All right."

"That's good." I tried to make my voice sound drawn out and tough, like Suzanne's.

A door slammed shut on her end. "That's my father," Charlotte said. "He just got off of work."

"Oh." Then: "My father's still at work."

"Oh."

"So—uh—how's school?"

"It sucks," Charlotte said.

"Really?"

"Sucks." There was the very faint sound of static on the line. "Listen," she said, "I better get going. My father doesn't like me talking on the phone too much."

The telephone rings again. My thoughts have not been traveling quickly enough: I am making them fly now, not just floating them gently through the air. Quick, quick, hang up the telephone, hang it up, just— whoever you are, just—

My father strides to the telephone. "Suzanne is eating her dinner," he shouts and slams the receiver down into its cradle.

"What was that?" Suzanne asks.

"One of your punk boyfriends."

"Who?"

"How the hell should I know? You're running around with half the creeps in this town."

"Josh," my mother says.

"Don't you Josh me." He draws his breath in sharp and long, so long I think he will suck all the air out of this room.

"Daddy," Suzanne says, "I'm not running around with—"

"Don't tell me what you're doing. I know what you're doing. I know what you are."

"I'm not."

"I know what you are."

"You're crazy," Suzanne says.

My throat is so tight that my food cannot go down. I lift my napkin to my lips and spit a half-chewed piece of meat into it. "I don't feel—" I say, shoving my napkin under my plate and standing. "May I be excused—"

I swing myself up the stairs, two at a time. At the top, I hear his footsteps coming after me.

In my room, I scurry under the blankets, pulling them up over my head. The air inside this tent of flannel is musty and good.

"You—" he says. "Look at me." He shuts the door. "You know better than to act that way."

"I didn't feel well. I—"

"Shut up," he says. He sits down on the bed next to me. "Your old man tries. He's not such a bad guy," and his rough hand strokes my face. I shudder away from him.

"Goddamn you," he says. He crouches over me, fixes his hands around my throat.

"No. Let . . ." I try to say, but my words are lost, unable to pass the grip of his hands. I am falling, swirling downwards although still on the bed. Cannot stop and. In one thousand seven hundred and. Sixteen years. The strangeness is not conserved. In one.

He lets up the pressure for a second. "Mommy!" I scream.

The door opens. She is here. The light from the hallway is bright; I am safe. In one thousand seven hundred and fifty-seven days I will be sixteen years old.

"What did you do that for?" he shouts. "This has nothing to do with her."

"Mommy," I cry.

Her arms are folded across her chest. All I can ask is that she rescue me. I cannot ask for her comfort. "Kate," she says. "You shouldn't upset your father . . ."

Monday morning, I get down to the kitchen before anybody else. My mother's mixing orange juice. Very casually, I ask her: "Who's Dr. Fishbien?"

She doesn't say anything.

"He sends bills to Daddy."

"You know better than to read other people's mail."

I snort. "I knew you weren't supposed to read the *inside*. I didn't know it was a crime to read the outside."

She walks over to the clothes dryer in the corner of the kitchen, picks up a stack of folded clothes, and walks out of the room. I swear to God if my mother ever found out that the Russians were about to drop the Bomb, she'd start putting my father's shorts away in his drawer. Really.

"What're you doing here?" Charlotte says to me when I get to homeroom.

"Huh?"

"Aren't you Jewish?"

"No."

"Ooohh," she says, "I didn't know you were Catholic."

"I'm not."

"What are you?"

"Nothing," I say.

"*Nothing*? You've got to be something."

"We don't go to church," I say.

"But you've got to *be* something."

I shrug.

First period is English class. There are thirty desks in this classroom, in rows six across and five deep. Twenty-nine of them are empty. It's Yom Kippur. I'm in the smart class. All the other smart kids are Jewish.

"Your mother wouldn't let you bunk today, huh?" Mr. Dolan says.

"No, sir."

"You know, if you weren't here I could go down to the teachers' room and smoke a cigarette."

"Oh."

When I get home from school, there's another bill from Dr. Fishbien. And no one else is home—my parents are both at work; Suzanne's out— she's always out; Rebecca's wracking up her extra-curricular activities that she can list on her college applications; Jimmy's playing hockey in the muddy vacant lot two blocks away.

I put the kettle on the stove to boil. I learned this trick on *Love of Life*—my favorite of all the soap operas I watched last summer when I was in the hospital.

When it boils, I hold Dr. Fishbien's bill in the jet of steam. My hands turn red and sting from the heat. The paper wrinkles, growing damp. Should I try to pull it open now? Suppose I do and it's not ready, the paper rips? I could always throw it away, in the bottom of the wastebasket. My father would think it had gotten lost in the mail.

Gently, I edge my finger under the flap. It gives way easily, almost miraculously.

I am holding the piece of paper in my hand, unfolding it: "Office visits: October 2, 9, 16, 23, 30 @ $35 $175." I fold the paper up quickly, stick it back in the envelope, press down the flap. I thought it would say what it was for. $175, in one month. Where does he get that much money? Something must really be wrong with him. Maybe a brain tumor, like in *Death Be Not Proud*. Maybe cancer.

I've made a resolution. I've decided to stop being such a klutz and always getting flack from everyone because I'm not clean enough, because I don't smell the right way, because my braces clunk, because I don't have any friends. Not that I'm planning to give up anything—get a Ph.D. in giggling or anything like that—just that I'm going to start being more normal.

So this morning, I went down to the drugstore and bought a copy of *Young Teen* magazine. Suzanne says that the only people who read magazines written for teenagers are the real losers and she would not be "caught dead"—her exact words—reading them. But then, she doesn't need to—she already knows everything you're supposed to do and not supposed to do, and how to dress and have friends.

The first thing I turn to is the Fashion Hints column—I figure I need help in that department. In the Fashion Hints column you write a letter and tell them what your particular fashion problem is and they answer it for you. The first letter is from someone with short legs who wants to know what kind of clothing would be "most flattering." The Fashion Editor tells her that she's in luck—the new empire dresses that flair out from beneath the bustline are just perfect for girls with short legs.

"Dear Fashion Editor," I could write, "my problem is that I wear braces on both my legs and walk with crutches. When I get dressed up nicely, I look like a robot in a party dress. Any fashion suggestions?"

You're in luck. The fashion shows in Paris this year featured the metal look. It hasn't hit these shores yet, but within a year the other girls at school will be dressing themselves up in aluminum foil and carrying purses made of steel girders—and casting jealous eyes at your high-grade aluminum and anodized steel. SO just hold on for a little bit more, and you'll be right in the swing of things!

Or maybe:

Might we suggest a tent? It's not nearly as uncomfortable as it sounds—you just cut a hole for your head in the top and leave out the stakes and poles. Step inside, zip it up, and all your problems will be discreetly hidden. And don't think that just because you have to wear a tent you'll be stuck in drab browns and khakis—L. L. Bean has a great new line that comes in fashionable reds, yellows, and blues!

I know what I'd really get. True beauty shines from within. Wear a pleasant smile and clothes that are wrinkle free. Avoid loud prints. Take part in a lot of afterschool activities.

And then, I see this announcement: "Just published! *Young Teen*'s informative new booklet, "Facts about Love and Sex for Teens . . ." I don't need to read anymore: I put my fifty cents in an envelope and send away for it.

The kids are asleep. Dave and Trina (who absolutely won't *allow* you to call them "Mr. & Mrs. Sandersen," perish the thought) have gone out with my parents.

Dave is a pretty sad case, if you ask me. He has this moustache. One time I got here a few minutes early, and as I'm coming up the walk I see him sitting in the living room with this stupid little brush in his hand, combing his moustache. He sees me and dips it into his pocket, real quick. Uh-oh, the babysitter caught me brushing my moustache. Come on.

You really get to know people when you babysit for them. Not that I go snooping in people's drawers or anything like that. I've only done that a couple of times. Dave is a real pseud. He has this copy of *Playboy* magazine sitting on his coffee table. I just know that when people see it there he says, "Oh, I just bought that because I wanted to read the interview with Thelonious Monk." Sure you did, Dave.

Plus, downstairs he has all these books that sound dirty but aren't. He's got this one called *Eros and Civilization* which I thought was going to be pretty hot. I picked it up and got treated to: "At the same time, however, the sexual relations themselves become more closely assimilated with social relations; sexual liberty is harmonized with profitable conformity." I'm not kidding. The whole book was like that.

But upstairs, Dave has all his real dirty books. Upstairs, where his hot-shot lawyer and architect and doctor friends won't see them. Even then, he never goes out and buys the real honest raunch-o stuff like they have behind the counter at Izzie's. Oh, no. He's got these books that have introductions by some guy with a Ph.D. in psychology that says how this book is full of redeeming social value because it points out how awful it is to be a loose woman. Or else they have the woman do all this wild stuff and then in the last chapter she becomes a nun or a missionary to Africa or something. The only problem with these books is that you never find out what people actually do. You know what I mean. Everyone pants and moans but they never actually describe the whole thing.

Dave and Trina and my folks come rolling in around midnight. Trina's laughing: they must have stopped off at a club—*i.e.*, a bar. "Stay and have another drink," Trina's saying to my folks. I'm putting on my jacket, hoping that they're not so drunk they'll forget to pay me. My father picks up *Playboy*.

"There's a good article in there about—," Dave says.

"I don't want to read any article," my father says. "I just want to look at the tits."

"Josh," my mother says.

I flop myself down across my bed, pick up my copy of *Young Teen*. Here's an article on how to shop for your new fall fashion wardrobe—I can skip that. The way I shop for my new fall fashion wardrobe is that I go into Suzanne's room and she goes through her closet and says, "I hate this," and throws the offending garment on the bed; "I *never* wear this," and that gets tossed onto the heap. *Voilà*, my fall wardrobe.

"Modess Because . . ." and underneath there's a picture of this beautiful girl in her prom gown. "Problem Fingernails?" "Invite the whole crowd over for a big autumn bash!" And there's a two-page color spread of all these moronically happy young teens dancing, laughing, talking, snacking. (I could invite my whole crowd over for a big bash and still have plenty of room left over for the Rhode Island Philharmonic Orchestra.)

In the back there's this column called "Problems of Young Living." It begins with this letter from a thirteen year old who's having problems getting along with her parents; lives on a farm and has to get up at 4 A.M. to do chores, they're so strict and blah, blah, blah. The Problems of Young Living Editor suggests that she talk to her doctor or minister. Then there's one from some poor dork who's just moved to a new town and doesn't have any friends. The answer lady says: "You say no one ever invites you *anyplace*. Have you tried inviting *them*? Strike up a conversation with someone interesting and then say: 'How about a game of tennis this afternoon?'"

I come downstairs a little before dinner time. My mother is pouring frozen peas into boiling water. Thin strips of bacon are frying in the skillet. This is the food we eat when my father is not coming home for dinner: bacon, eggs, leftovers. Tuesday night, when he has a late class and eats at school, is "clean out the refrigerator night." My mother sets in front of us leftover broccoli and wilted salad, an odd lamb chop or two congealed in its pale fat, barely warmed white rice. But this is not Tuesday. And my mother's eyes are rimmed with red.

"What's wrong?"

"Nothing's wrong," she says. "Everything's fine. Fine. Dinner. Call your sisters and brother."

"Where's Daddy?" Jimmy asks when we are all seated around the kitchen table.

"He's not going to be here for dinner tonight," my mother says.

"How come?" Jimmy asks.

"I'm going to do a project for the science fair," I say. "I think something about the Sargasso Sea."

"'Your mind and you are our Sargasso Sea . . .'" my mother says, tilting her head into the air the way she always does when she's delivering a quote.

"Where's Daddy?" Suzanne asks.

My mother lays her knife and fork down. She opens her mouth to speak; a tear runs down her cheek. "Your father," she says, and then rises, walking to the corner of the counter where the Kleenexes are kept, pulling out one and then another, "Your father's been under a lot of pressure lately. He—he's gone away for a rest."

"Where?" Suzanne asks.

"Well," my mother says, clearing her throat. "It's not exactly a hospital."

"Exactly what is it?" Suzanne asks.

"It's a place where people can go and rest for a while, get away from their problems."

I imagine a resort somewhere, the South Seas, perhaps, a ramshackle hotel in the background, like the one on *Adventures in Paradise* where tired men lie all day in hammocks, eased by tropical breezes, drinking sweet cocktails from the hollowed-out shells of pineapples.

"Butler?" Suzanne asks.

"Yes," my mother says softly. "Butler."

Butler? That is the nut house, the funny farm, the looney bin.

"The Sargasso Sea is actually a marine desert," I say. "Isn't that—"

Suzanne glares at me: "Would you shut up?"

After I take a shower and wash my hair, I wrap my head in a towel. I look at myself in the mirror—with my hair wrapped up in this turban I look very old—seventeen, or maybe even twenty. I hold an imaginary cigarette at a jaunty angle. I am sitting in the Deux Maggots, talking with my good friends, Jean-Paul and Simone. "My mother's a professor." I take a long inhale: "And my father's a madman."

Didn't sound quite right. I try it again, staring full at my face in the mirror: "My father's a madman."

"Who the hell are you talking to?" Suzanne hollers.

I open the door, stick my head out, and shout quickly back: "I'm practicing a book report."

I flop myself across the bed, start reading "Facts about Love and Sex for Teens," which just arrived in the mail today. I don't want you to think I'm a sex maniac or anything—I just want to know a few things. Like what happens when people do it—I mean besides all the moaning and gasping with pleasure.

"Facts about Love and Sex for Teens" begins with a rundown about the old Curse and how it's "not an unpleasant event in a girl's life" (could have fooled me); I'm skimming along, trying to find the good stuff. Here it is: "Sexual intercourse is a time of great sharing and love between two married people." That's it. I can't believe it. Fifty cents. Fifty cents for that.

"Hey," Charlotte says, "will you do me a favor? I got this catechism test tomorrow. Ask me the questions out of this book—see if I know the answers."

She hands me this blue-and-white book that's got all these drawings of Jesus and angels with haloes floating through the sky.

"Just flip through," she says. "I've got to know *everything.*"

"'Why are we on earth?'" I begin, a question I've often asked myself.

"We are on earth," Charlotte recites, eyes rolled towards the ceiling, "to learn to know God," she ticks off one finger, "to love and to serve Him," she ticks off her next finger, "and one day to live with Him forever."

"Right." I'm impressed. "'How did suffering and death come into the world?'"

"Suffering and death came into the world through sin."

"But how did sin come into the world?"

"Is that in the book?" Charlotte asks.

"Sorry. 'Why does God allow us to suffer?'"

"God permits us to suffer because through suffering he wants to lead us to salvation."

"Manic-depressive psychosis," my mother says, as she presses her foot down on the brake. "A chemical imbalance in his brain." She slows the station wagon almost to a stop and we ease over the bump in the drive. Oh, no, there is nothing really wrong with him; just a few chemicals off-kilter, just something in his head a little out of whack. Everything is going to be just fine and dandy!

Butler is green lawns and soft footsteps, a red brick building gloomy in front of us. My father bumbles down the steps: he is shaking, ever so slightly, shaking; a wide grin slices across his face.

"Rebecca couldn't come," my mother says. "She had a yearbook meeting."

"A yearbook meeting," my father says, nodding his head up and down.

"Yes," Suzanne says, "a yearbook meeting."

I wait for my father's anger to lash out, but he is groggy, nodding his head.

"Lithium," my father says when we are sitting on the grass. "They say it's a miracle drug."

"Remember when they invented penicillin," my mother says, smiling, smiling, "and suddenly *all* those diseases . . ."

"That's what they say. A miracle."

"What do you do all day, Daddy?" Jimmy asks.

"Well, we get up in the morning and have breakfast."

"Breakfast in bed?" my mother asks.

"Yes, in bed."

"That must be fun," she says.

"Then we have O.T., occupational therapy. I painted a picture. Of that tree," he says, pointing, "and then. Sometimes. You wonder if there's anything they can do for you. You wonder if . . ." and my father, sitting on the grass, draws his knees up towards his chest, wrapping his arms around them, and slowly begins to rock back and forth.

Dear Problems of Young Living Editor:

I do not have a real problem that I need your help with; I just have a few questions I would like answered. Also, I know that you "regret you cannot answer letters individually" but I thought maybe you could, just this once. I really do need to know the answers to these questions and if you published this in Young Teen *then anybody who knew me would realize this was from me. I've enclosed a stamped self-addressed envelope.*

What does manic-depressive psychosis mean? Why are we on earth? Why does my mother always start folding laundry when I want to talk to her? What does 'Like the hully-gully but not so slow' mean? (This is part of a song I hear coming from my sister's radio.)

Also, I sent away for your booklet called, "Facts about Love and Sex for Teens" and while I certainly appreciated all the valuable information there are a few more things I would like to know. (I suppose I should tell you here that even though I'm only eleven I'm very mature for my age; I have a very high IQ and skipped third grade and am in junior high school already.) My question is this: when people have "intercourse" what actually happens? How long does it last? Why is it done in bed? Please don't tell me to talk to our clergyman, because we don't go to church, or to my family doctor, because he looks like Frankenstein and is a real creep. I really do need to know the answers to these questions.

My sister Suzanne used to be a regular person, I mean she read books and talked in a normal tone of voice but ever since she turned thirteen she's been really dopey, baby talking, etc. Will this happen to me?

My Family Is Unhappy

My mother is unhappy. She wants more. The more she gets the more she wants. She wants my sister to be happy. My sister is unhappy. She is getting a divorce and her legs swell. She takes pills for her legs but they still swell. She has tests. She is living with an older man, a fact which makes my mother unhappy. My mother wants her children to marry rich men. She wants grandchildren who are happy. My sister will probably never have children. My mother is a child. My father is unhappy. My mother thinks he has underachieved, as has she by marrying him. We are all lazy and underachievers. We all think about what we could have been. My father is unhappy because my mother is not happy with what he has achieved. He makes money. He lies to her because she does not think he makes enough money. She is jealous of her rich friends. My father is lazy. He has no hobbies and does not cut the grass himself, but he works long hours and is most happy at his job. He is afraid of dying. My mother and father are in love. I am in love with a married man. I am in love with a divorced man who will probably never remarry and I am in love with a man who will probably never marry. I am also in love with a gay man. These affairs make my mother unhappy because it seems I will never marry and have children. She wants me to marry a rich man who, she says, is as easy to love as a poor man. She says I should understand this better now that I am older and realize that life is no bed of roses. I understand that and don't understand why I choose these men. But one has nothing to do with the other. Perhaps it is because I am lazy. I work hard but that is easy. I take my love affairs seriously but that is easy. I have no hobbies. My sister has many hobbies and is always buying new tools for the latest of them. She has only one lover and a husband she is divorcing. She learns quickly but gives up easily. Her house is full of discarded tools. I do not give up but that is easy for me. I do not give up easily. I hold on. I make my family think I am happy. It is easier to make them think I work hard, am happy in the life I have created (and I make them think I have created my life), than to let them know that I am as unhappy and lazy and swollen as they. The unhappier they are, the happier I make them think I am. I am a bundle of joy, the first born, laughing on the middle of the bed they still sleep in (no, that's my sister). I am a bundle of joy, the second born, laughing and running on the beach, so cute the photographer just had to shoot me.

II

The beach is in Atlantic City. We spend our summers in a rented cottage with blue hydrangeas. It is really Marvin Gardens and not Atlantic City. I am eight years old and I think I have gotten ugly. My sister thinks she is ugly. Everyone tells us we're beautiful. My grandmother lives with us in the rented cottage and my father drives down on weekends. My grandfather has died. My sister is twelve. My sister hates me. I want her to love me though I don't like her. She tickles me, not in fun but to make me cry. I think I am fat. She reads books and gets a better suntan. She thinks I am prettier than she. She is riding on a Public Service bus from Atlantic City to Philadelphia with my mother. It is raining and the bus crashes into a truck. My sister's legs are crushed. My mother tells me my sister will not be home for a long time. She tells me this much later because she is also in the hospital with internal injuries. My cousin Doris who is fifteen and not very pretty comes to Marvin Gardens to take care of me. We play Chutes and Ladders and go to the movies when it rains. I can't remember what the house looked like. We rent a different one each summer. There is a restaurant near the beach with good minute steak sandwiches. I like to go up the chutes and down the ladders when Doris won't play with me anymore. In a photograph my sister is sitting on the beach, her back to the camera. She has pigtails and her legs are stretched out at angles. This is the last picture of her before the accident. She has strong legs and a strong back. I am digging in the sand with my bucket.

III

My mother and father are taking a vacation alone for the first time since we were born. We always take trips together, putting an extra cot in the motel room. They say parents who travel without their children are selfish, that children need to learn how other people live, to see the world. My parents are going to Puerto Rico and I am staying home. My sister is still in the hospital. My grandmother will take care of me. My mother and father say they don't know how parents can sleep in air-conditioned bedrooms while their children swelter. This seems true to me and I am proud of them for knowing how children feel. They buy an air conditioner and give me their big beige fan. They don't have money for two air conditioners, but I can spread the green mat that belonged to my grandfather at the foot of their bed and sleep there. I don't like sleeping on the floor.

IV

My mother and father bring back four thick brown-and-white towels that have the letters E D in fancy script. They stole the towels from the El Dorado Hotel in Puerto Rico. They are the biggest, thickest towels I've ever seen and I am proud of them. Sixteen years later one towel is left. My mother takes care of her things. Sixteen years later I see a man wearing blue trunks on Jones Beach. He is sitting on an El Dorado towel. He seems like a careful man. I want to ask him if he met my mother and father in Puerto Rico. My mother and father went to Puerto Rico because her uterus flipped over and had to be removed. It made her sick.

V

The car is filled with gray trapped smoke. It is raining and the windows are rolled up. We are driving to Atlantic City in November to see my sister at the Children's Seashore House. I am not yet twelve, I am not even eleven, but I don't know how old I am. My mother and father are smoking cigarettes. I hate my sister. I have a headache. I can't go past the waiting room with green walls. Slowly my sister is wheeled into the doorway. She has pimples. We take a walk on the boardwalk in the light rain. It is empty except for a few other children from the Seashore House on crutches or in wheelchairs. I don't remember what we say. I want to be pushed in the wheelchair. I want my sister to walk. She is getting all the attention and I must not complain. I am selfish to complain. I can walk and she cannot. How would I like it? But I don't know what it's like. I am too young to go past the waiting room, too young to see the whirlpool baths and exercise machines. I am fascinated by the idea of them and think it might be nice. I have no right to think that. It is bad. I am lucky to be able to walk. My sister gives my mother a wooden basket burned with a red rose. She is learning to play the guitar. Everyone says she is brilliant and brave. I am sweet and pretty and have no gifts to bring home. I am sweet and I hate my sister and know that I am prettier than she. She is brilliant and brave, a miracle of science. Her arms are thin and covered with hair. She is ugly, she is ugly. I am sweet.

VI

In the photograph my sister is lying on the green chaise lounge in the middle of the living room. This is where she lives now. She is skinny with greasy black hair. You can see her pimples. I don't remember if she is smiling. Everyone comes to her on the chaise lounge. My sister cannot walk. She cannot go to the bathroom. My mother brings her a pan. My mother washes her in a pan. My sister is playing the guitar. Teachers come to her. She is learning Spanish. She looks Spanish. Her legs are covered with a sheet and blanket. Under them are her legs, wrapped in bandages, straight out and skinnier than the rest of her. There are worms in her legs. The worms eat dead tissue. My mother doesn't tell me because she doesn't want to upset me. She changes the bandages. Sometimes my mother throws up in the bathroom after she has changed my sister's bandages,

but I don't know why. I think it is because she is unhappy. I run in and out
of the house and say hello to my sister. She hates me. I didn't know if she
hated me when she was in the hospital. Now I know. She hates me because I can walk. She says I was born under a lucky star, even though she
is smarter. In my room I look out the window trying to find the star, but
they all look alike. I wish I lived in the living room on the green chaise
with my teachers coming to me.

VII

My sister goes back to high school in the tenth grade. She wears leg
braces and tries to look like the other kids. She wears a white pleated
arnyl skirt. In biology class Ellen Gambol, who sits behind my sister,
wipes her feet on it. My sister's hair is still greasy. My mother, sister, and I
sit on my sister's bed with the green spread. First my sister cries, then I
cry, then my mother cries. We can't stop. Ellen Gambol's sister, Debbie, is
in my class. I think I should hate her but it is not Debbie's fault. She always asks how my sister is doing. My sister goes to the junior prom with
Eddie Schwartz, who goes to another school. She wears a white strapless
dress she and my mother chose with great care. My father takes a photograph in front of the fireplace. I ask my sister if she had a good time. She
says, Not really.

VIII

My sister goes to college. I think she is a beatnik. She wears black sweaters, has long black hair, plays the guitar, and speaks Spanish. Her college
is in New York City and is built on high cliffs called Palisades. I take pride
in being able to tell people which campus she attends. I do not know anything else about her, except that she is different and for the first time it
seems okay. Uptown, I say.

IX

She is getting married. She is buying dresses with small floral prints. She
has a big diamond. He is graduating from Amherst. He went to Exeter, a
boarding school for rich boys. He has freckles and sunburns easily. He is
making my sister unhappy. I shout at him, You have no right to make
my sister unhappy. She's been unhappy all her life. He is leaning against
my sister's green bookcase. I am crying and can't stop. My sister is crying.
She says, I didn't think you loved me. I tell her I love her. She says she loves
me. They get married the next day at the Quaker Meeting House. They
move to a house with its own name. I take pride in telling people the
name of my sister's house. My sister's legs are always swollen. She is trying
not to be different. My sister leaves one night. She says her husband is
crazy and everyone says so. He hit her and she almost fell. She takes the

cats. He steals them back. She takes the cats. I don't know who has the photographs of my sister dressed in a white gown, her black hair long and straight. My sister tells lies. She says she blacks out. She says she tried to cut her wrists. My father will not speak to her. My mother is unhappy. My sister says she hates my mother and father. She has opened an Indian jewelry shop. She says she is an Indian. She visits my mother and father for six weeks. When I ask if she had a good time, she says, Not really. My sister is a liar. My sister is unhappy. Perhaps she likes being unhappy. She sews, plays the guitar, takes photographs, speaks Spanish, Russian, makes silver jewelry, knits. She thinks I am more talented than she. I think she is more exotic than I. She is envious of my legs. I am envious of her unique childhood. On the day of the accident, my mother was taking my sister to a child psychiatrist because she was unhappy and had been torturing me excessively.

The Wrestled Angel

The stories and poems in "The Wrestled Angel" concern the struggles that disability calls forth. In his poem "The Sentry of Portoferraio" Epstein ponders the purpose of the disabled. Are they portent or scapegoat or foil against which the rest of us measure the beauty of well-functioning bodies? In "Black Lightning" Arthur Sze identifies with the blind girl typing braille. Barbara Howes' poem "The Lace Maker" describes the frustrations of dim or failing sight. The excerpt from the novel *Down All the Days* by Christy Brown, himself a severely disabled victim of cerebral palsy, dramatizes the awakening of the senses to the beauty and terror of life, the mystery of sex, the struggles of his parents. "Awakened as any animal, and more immensely mute, he was learning to live and give without being blinded by the stars." In "The Freaks at Spurgin Road Field," Richard Hugo ruminates about the attitude toward the handicapped of the so-called normal world. "Finch the Spastic Speaks" shows a man who would be known—by others and by himself—as more than a brilliant freak.

The Sentry of Portoferraio

Blame this island town for the broken boy
who keeps his watch high on the falcon fortress.
Blame this town of rose and sea-green stone
stairways, and the daredevil swallows.
Was it not enough that beneath a circus of birds
his eyes should blindly fix upon each other?
Born lame as an old joke
did he have to grow up in such a town
of pinnacles, one cocked leg
cursing the steps that lead him to his home?

Accuse the snake in the cactus, fig, and grape
gathering liquor from the rainless air;
scold fish heads in the monger's stall,
cats on the sill. Charge the parents
of sturdy children whose eyes renew the horizon,
whose legs conquer mountains and pines.
Did we not conspire in narrow prayers
to divide his share of health among us?
Did we not invest in our cross-eyed sentry
suffering enough to make a nation wise?

It is the fury of providence
to crowd a family of pain into one creature,
then crown him guardian angel of a town.
It is his lonely insistence on Heaven
that leads lovers to the sudden view
of their bodies broken beautifully against themselves,
that leads our village skyward to command
an ocean, rise and stand up to the sun!
But somebody has to pay for the hobbling climb,
somebody has to pay for his double vision.

Black Lightning

A blind girl
stares at me,
then types out ten lines
in braille.

The air has a scent
of sandalwood and
arsenic; a night-blooming cereus
blooms on a dark path.

I look at the
short and long flow
of the lines:
and guess at garlic,
the sun, a silver desert rain,
and palms.

Or is it simply
about hands, a river of light,
the ear of a snail,
or rags?

And, stunned, I feel
the nerves of my hand flashing
in the dark, feel
the world as black
lightning.

The Lace Maker

Needle, needle, open up
The convolvulus of your eye,
I must come upon it quick
Or my thread will die.

Night is settling down outside,
My sallow candle seems to thin,
But I must weave this laddered thread
To nest each rare space in.

It is dark. Darkness plaits a scarf
Over my eyes. Can finger sprout
Eyes at the tip to guide its work?
Each evening, I go out

To Sainte Gudule—if I can see
Needlepoint of aspiring stone,
The window's rose embroidery
Trained like a trumpet upon Heaven,

Then I may live; but if my sight
Narrows toward death, a black-avised
Gargoyle will jut out, grinning there,
Exulting in that swirling mist.

Lying Alone in the Dismal Winter Mornings

Lying alone in the dismal winter mornings under the rough blankets and coats after his brothers had gone downstairs to breakfast and away up the bitter windy street to school, he would get once more the heavy under-the-blankets animal-human smell lingering, lingering from the night before and the queer dead-of-night furtive fumblings and stifled moans and groans of one of his brothers whispering some day-long-known girl's name, unknowing of him who lay sleepless and quickly alive to pain in his own wrinkled corner of the vast floor mattress. More and more often now the same contortions would precede the dawning juices and secretions that splashed forth from his own body on the rim of some fabulous and erotic vision in warm jerked-out gushes mingled with horrific shame and defiant delight, lacerating his wavering, quavering new-from-the-depths senses with bold knife-strokes of pleasure, the exultant fierce leap into estranged ecstasy, the volcanic shuddering in all parts of him, the bewildered breathless animal noises emitted in a swift timeless suspension of thought. Then the gradual sinking back, the long drop down the chill cheerless stair of inexorable returning reality, the deadly familiar proportions, shapes and outlines of the room, the green distemper on the walls penknife-pricked with his brothers' names, the huge Sacred Heart over the bed, Christ the all-suffering beggar-man with blood-oozing palms outspread in that terrible gesture of mild-mannered meekness, the first faint fatal seeds of guilt making the secret victory of a moment ago a hot shame burning within and withering all sense of pleasure.

His own body became at this time a new and never-known landscape to him and avidly he explored, soaking up its smells and scenes and sensations, surprised or perplexed or disgusted constantly by what he discovered; the gradual presence of hair on his lower parts caused him quick fright and alarm so that he wanted to hide this curious body-grass from even his own eyes; yet as his sister one day combed before the mirror and under her raised arms he saw the fine dark under-hair a peculiar throb of pleasure gripped and held him, and it seemed cruel and barbaric when later she shaved her armpits with Father's safety blade, leaving the soft under-arm raw and pitted with tiny dark ugly pin-pricks where the soft dark sweat-limp hair had been.

He thought with almost affectionate pity of the doomed denizens of his own body, the valiant vermin spawned from his own sweat and dirt moving with infinite dignity and languor under his clothes, of the lumbering lice in his head creeping always in a dark jungle, each blade of hair looming before them like trunks of trees, threatened by the scythe stroke of scissors and cruel steel-toothed combs and murderous probing death-crushing fingernails at bathtime every Saturday night, fatal fellow-dwellers of his flesh.

The vast cloudless blue sky of smokeless summer days terrified him, as did everything of absolute petrified purity, a sky like the face of an idiot scrubbed clean and empty of all wit, anger, tenderness, desire, the pathetic human distortions and disfigurements that alone comforted and captivated him; a sky with nothing in it glaring down in pitiless abundance of power, dense and dead and pure, and the sun in that sky gleaming in the centre like the huge inflamed orifice of some unimagined monster; and summer was not always lovely. It opened up festering wounds and weeping sores in the earth, brought evil smells from decaying food in narrow dark-shadowed streets, made the grass wither and turn bilious yellow and the flowers to wilt, ravished of moisture or scent, on roadside hedges like powder puffs caked with dried powder, like biscuits in shop windows with little mounds of lard-like cream jellied and beleaguered by flies. Once returning from the canal they had come upon a cat dead on the road; somebody got a stick and turned it over gingerly and its ancient wrinkled face grinned and grimaced up at them; its belly was flat where the motor car wheel had gone over it and a few drops of blood were caked and hard on the rubbery skin; it had already begun to smell; the apples and pears in the orchard behind the high wall on the other side of the road glowed in green shadow.

At night, poised in that in-between-land of dream and wakefulness bordered but unclouded by sleep, he could look down to where he had left himself lying upon the great gaunt mattress, and be filled with baffled pity and rage for this lucid nakedness, the dark brown matted hair upon the pillow, the high-flung cheek bones in the skull-like face intent and brooding, inscrutably absent, implacably walled by the intense, absurd, aloof indwelling that dropped sheer as any cliff between himself and the awakening terrors of the touchable world; with a curious contortion of heart he saw the hollowed cheeks, the thin pale gauze of closed eyelid tinged with a bluish penumbra, pulsing minutely, the sleep-sweat around the rigid mouth and in the hollow of the jaw, the keen hawk-like arrogance of the features forever rapt on some perfect peak only he could see in that red-bramble land all soft and grey and fine and exquisite as dust and a cold blue splendour of moonlight everywhere and the nets of his wonder gathering dreams from nowhere.

After rain the broad road in front of the house would glisten and mirror the clouds scudding across the pale green evening sky like dark battalions of weirdly shaped horses; the concrete widths were no longer dull, but shone strange and misty like a lake, capturing the leaning shadows of houses looming on the far side of the street, the cars and buses and people passing on bicycles, broken into blurred fantastic images grotesque, unreal, without form, yet more real to him watching from the kitchen window than the houses, the vehicles, the people themselves. Shadows spoke more lucidly to his mind than the substance that caused them. He discerned a life and mystery, a uniqueness in them that he searched for but could never find in the bland open and forever closed faces of people and things. A world at once unknown but vastly knowable welled up to him out of reflected surfaces and textures, alive with magic shapes in which moved mysteries and meanings without a name, yet known to him immemorially, through the alchemy of thought, sense and dream forever returning and receding upon the fringes of his mind with the soft slap of surf lipping a fragile shore, a shell-deep echo of intimate gentle voices vouchsafing him peace and visitations of beauty in his islanded world. His far and fabulous angel would come, not with trumpets triumphant and tumultuous wings, but gently and with a gradual joy; aside and within, he listened for that presence.

The large, loose, knuckle-jointed, work-roughened hands of his father lying for a rare moment passive on dungareed knees or lap filled him with terror and yet a strange burning unnameable longing; he imagined those hands alert and agile with the bricklayer's trowel and chisel, flashing in the weak mocking winter sunshine on scaffolding high above the city, piling brick upon brick with brisk brave strokes, the sinewy wrist moving subtly, magically moulding a patchwork pyramid of cemented rectangles to enclose the lives, loves, labours, passions, despairs of innumerable strangers; those master-craftsman's hands turning deserts of empty spaces into jungles of human dwellings, offices, stores, theatres, churches, schools, hospitals, fun palaces, the desperate disarray or organized chaos and convoluted canyons where men and women worked, made love, bore children, longed for heights and strange lands and slowly ceased to dream through a myriad profusion of cement-dry days and nights punctuated by traffic screams and the wail of ships' sirens from the foggy river and feeling again with the far-off shrill of a train in the dark morning the loneliness of being on earth. The broad hands of his father had acted in the making of that immense outer wilderness of brick and block and solemn stone, and they were thus both ugly and beautiful in his eyes and eloquent and noble when, as often, they bled from the bitter winter frost, and ugly beyond endurance when they thundered upon the flesh of his mother and flayed her bestially. In dreams his father's hands floated eerily, mostly menacing and monstrous and falling upon him like flattened sheets of iron, but in rare instances stroking him too with marvellous gentleness and a tremulous strength.

Once, when he had seen his father touch his mother's hair almost timidly, a throb of joy and absurd ecstatic hope filled him; the moment burnt bright and perfect, full of a wild sweetness as when sometimes he fervently lost himself in prayer, the moment dropping into his mind like a first spring blossom; then almost instantly it was gone, broken, washed away on the harsh returning wave of his father's voice demanding his supper. Nothing of peace or charm lasted longer than it took his beating heart to feel it, and he was back once more in the walled garden of his thoughts, chasing the shadows of such moments, listening always rapt and intent for the wings of his ambiguous angel, the touch of felicitous fingers upon his brow that turned always and abruptly to a vicious cheek-stinging slap dashing the tears from his eyes.

Awkward as any animal, and more immensely mute, he was learning to grow and live without being blinded by the stars.

The Freaks at Spurgin Road Field

The dim boy claps because the others clap.
The polite word, handicapped, is muttered in the stands.
Isn't it wrong, the way the mind moves back.

One whole day I sit, contrite, dirt, L.A.
Union Station, '46, sweating through last night.
The dim boy claps because the others clap.

Score, 5 to 3. Pitcher fading badly in the heat.
Isn't it wrong to be or not be spastic?
Isn't it wrong, the way the mind moves back.

I'm laughing at a neighbor girl beaten to scream
by a savage father and I'm ashamed to look.
The dim boy claps because the others clap.

The score is always close, the rally always short.
I've left more wreckage than a quake.
Isn't it wrong, the way the mind moves back.

The afflicted never cheer in unison.
Isn't it wrong, the way the mind moves back
to stammering pastures where the picnic should have worked.
The dim boy claps because the others clap.

Finch the Spastic Speaks

The doctor's achievements with problems like mine are famous; his connection with the university—research and occasional lectures—accounts for my choice of this state, city, school. I had, of course, my pick of institutions. He is, I think, basically kind, but too great a scientist to obscure his ministrations with mercy or pity, and for this I am grateful. Though we have met each month for the past five years, we have no . . . what you would call *rapport*.

Answer a leading question: what is Finch? Is he the body, the badly made bundle of nerve cells and motor responses? Or is he the mind, the intelligence, the scholarships and fellowships, the heap of plaques, medallions, scrolls, given in testimony to his brilliance? Or is he something even more than these, a total greater than the sum of his parts? I ask you, does not Finch . . . feel?

Ah, you mock! Finch, you say, Finch of all people! Finch? Poor, pathetic Finch, with his tested and recorded intelligence quotient of two hundred and thirty-three, locked forever in his prison of chaotic muscles. Poor Finch, who falls as easily over a curbstone as an infant toddler over a toy. Unfortunate Finch, whose large, staring eyes often roll wildly behind his thick glasses. Tragic Finch, who must choke and strain like some strangling madman if he is to ask for so much as a drink of water.

You underestimate me.

Stripped to shorts and undershirt, I sit on the edge of the doctor's examination table, legs dangling. With an ordinary tape measure, he checks my calves, thighs, forearms, biceps, to see if any disparity has developed. Kneeling, he exerts pressure on each foot as I pull up against him, testing for any distinction in muscular strength. "Okey doke," he says, pausing to jot conclusions in the thick folder bearing my name that will doubtless one day yield monographs, to his ever-spreading renown. "Ready?" he says, handing pen and folder to the attentive nurse. I do not speak needlessly.

He stands near me, raises his hands, spreads his fingers like a wrestler coming to close with an opponent in the center of the ring. And I see it just that way, a contest, for my amusement. I am very strong.

Relaxation is the secret. I half-close my eyes to concentrate, bombarding my shoulders, arms, hands, fingers, with commands: relax! Gradually, the fingers twitch, release the edge of the table, and slowly my arms rise, fingers open to meet his. He meets me halfway, interlocks his

Reprinted by permission of Louisiana State University Press from *The Entombed Man of Thule* by Gordon Weaver; copyright © 1972.

fingers with mine, and we push, face to face. I watch his skin flush, eyes protrude ever so slightly, teeth clench. We push, as earnest as two fraternity boys arm wrestling for a pitcher of beer. I am very strong.

He grunts without meaning to, catches himself, pushes again, then gives up, exhales loudly. "Okay," he says. I smell the aroma of some candied lozenge on his breath. Is there a trace of sweat on his tanned brow? "Okay," he says, "okay now." To save time, the nurse helps him unlace our fingers.

There was an impressive formal reception when I came to the university, five years ago. Not for me alone, of course. Invited were perhaps a hundred new students with some claim to distinction: merit scholars, recipients of industrial science fellowships, national prize-winning essayists, valedictorians in great number. But, except for a small covey of timid and meticulous Negro boys and girls, to whom all the dignitaries paid solemn if perfunctory court, I was easily the center of attention.

Imagine Finch, the spastic, dressed for the occasion. (The habitual fraternity jacket was not to come until my sophomore year, when Delta Sigma Kappa, campus jocks, coming to know me from my work at the gymnasium, adopted me as something of a mascot, perhaps their social service project for the year—the jacket was free, as are the passes to football and basketball games. I could, if I cared to, sit on the players' bench.) I wear a dark suit with vest, and the dormitory housemother has tied a neat, hard little knot in my tie for me. I stand near the refreshment table, as erect as my balance will permit. My left arm is locked into place, palm up, whereon I place a napkin, saucer, and a clear glass cup of red punch which I have no interest in tasting. With utmost care, I have tenderly grasped the cup's handle between thumb and forefinger, and there I stand, listening, questioning, answering, discussing (I speak extraordinarily well this day!) with a crowd of deans, departmental chairmen, senior professors, polite faculty wives, the president of the student body, and a handful of upper-class and graduate honor students. From time to time a few wander away to make a ritual obeisance to the Negroes, but they return.

Finch, Finch is the main attraction! Finch, with his certified intelligence quotient of two hundred and thirty-three, Finch who probes and reveals yawning gaps in the reading of graduate students ten years his senior, Finch who speaks with authority of science, literature, and contemporary politics, Finch who dares to contradict the holder of the endowed chair in history! Oh, there is glory in this! Finch, who cannot tie a shoelace, cannot safely strike a match, has trouble inserting dimes in vending machine slots—Finch is master here!

The other new students stand on the fringe of my audience, bewildered, or stroll off to stare dumbly at the obligatory portraits of past university presidents and trustees that dot the walls. I grow weary, but the tremor of my head can pass for judicious nodding, the tick in my cheek for chewing gum. The punch in my cup rocks a little. Who is the free man here?

Is it the scholar-professor who must think hard to recall specific points in his dissertation if he is to answer me? Is it the hatchet-faced, balding Dean of Letters and Science who carefully defends the university against its out-of-state rival, which also sought Finch? Is it the beautiful girl who won a regional science fair, but stands here, open-mouthed and silent as Finch explicates the relationship between set theory and symbolic logic? Is it the faculty wife with bleached hair, calculating her sitter's wages, who dares not depart for fear of offending Finch? Or is it Finch, whose brain roars with commands of discipline to his muscles, achieved only with the excruciating tenuous force of his will?

What you might think a disaster was actually the climax of my triumph. I had almost no warning. I felt the spasm that plunged my chin down against my chest, felt a stiffening come over my arms and hands, but no more. As nicely as if I wished it, I tossed my cup of punch up and back over my shoulder, while the saucer snapped in two in my left hand, giving me a rather nasty cut across the palm. There was a fine spray of punch in the air, the cup shattering harmlessly against the wainscotted wall behind me. Only the beautiful winner of the regional science fair forgot herself so far as to shriek as if she had been goosed.

I allowed no time for tension or embarrassment. I spoke quickly, clear as a bell, "Please excuse me," and reached up with the napkin to wipe punch from my forehead and hair. I asked for a chair, was seated, and the conversation continued as before while my hand was bandaged.

Which of you, I ask, would dare such a thing outside your dreams? When I smiled they laughed. And the winner of the science fair blushed, mortified by her outburst, as I related other such experiences in my past for their entertainment.

Above all, do not underestimate me.

The doctor breathes heavily. At my sides, my hands still hold their clawlike, grappling shape. A small victory, I am stronger than he; something to savor for a short time each month. He writes again, says, "I trust you're keeping up with the schedule." I nod, or what passes for a nod. The nurse helps me into my shirt and trousers.

"I can't emphasize that enough, James," the doctor said. He has called me by my first name since I met him; I was, after all, only seventeen when my parents arranged the first consultation.

"I don't want to alarm you," he said, "but there is evidence of unilateral deterioration—" I know the jargon as well as he—"your right side's progressing fairly rapidly. I want you to stay with the schedule, and don't miss the medication. I'm going to write to your folks . . ."

I have always kept the schedule. Ever since I can remember, there has been a schedule, exercises, work with weights, isometrics, special breathing and relaxation drills. At home, in my dormitory room, in classes, on regular visits to the gymnasium, I have faithfully kept the schedule. And medication. Pills, occasional injections as new serums and theories prevail. My wristwatch is equipped with a small but persistent buzzer to keep me precisely on the schedule.

"You know the literature on progression yourself . . ." he is saying. The nurse is fastening the buckles on my shoes; I once counted it a great breakthrough to go from snaps to buckles. I looked forward to laces, but no longer care about such matters. The nurse brings my fraternity jacket.

"You do understand the import of what I'm saying, James?" the doctor said. I realized he wanted more than a nod or flutter of eyelids. I must speak.

I did not forget the beautiful winner of the regional science fair. I saw her now and again during my first quarter at the university. We passed in corridors, joined the same lines in the cafeteria and bookstore, and, once, sat in the same aisle in the auditorium to watch a foreign film. Whether she seemed to notice me or not (how, I ask, does one *not notice* Finch?), I never forgot her face as I saw it when my hand was being bandaged at the reception, flushed with distress for her unmannerly and callous shriek at my misfortune with the punch cup. I understood she was emotionally in my debt until I should release her.

As these weeks passed, I began to pay attention, to sometimes go out of my way to meet her as she left a class or walked one of the narrow paths crossing the wide, green campus on her way to or from her dormitory. I found stations, fixed and concealed points, from which to observe her at length. It was not until the first long vacation, however, that I recognized how affected I was by her beauty. Her name was Ellen.

Picture Finch: his father or mother drives him to the public library for a day's work, and he burrows into his books and three-by-five notecards with a determination the envy of any serious scholar. A librarian helps him carry books to a far, quiet corner near a window, where the sun's warm rays belie the frozen, cold stillness of the snow-covered streets and buildings outside. He begins, reads, writes, outlines, and time passes without his knowing it, or caring. But a dingy cloud throws him into shade, or the day has already faded to that dark, chill cast that is a deep winter afternoon. He lifts his trembling head, closes his eyes, sore with strain, and suddenly sees nothing, thinks of nothing, but the beautiful Ellen. History or political science or biology evaporate, and his reality consists only of her pale blond hair, the hazel tint of her bright, large eyes, the unbelievably fresh smoothness of her skin, the light downy hair on her arm, the sparkle of her white, even teeth; to the exclusion of even his life-long awareness of his insane, spastic body, Finch knows only this beautiful Ellen!

I see, I *feel* the beauty of her movement: her hand glides to gesture, her fingers curl around a pencil, artless as the flow of water, no more self-conscious than the law of gravity; her head tilts, or she throws it to cast her hair back out of her eyes; she sits, crosses one long, sleek leg over the other, and it bobs in time to the animation of her conversation; she arches her back, thrusts out her breasts, and lets her coat slide down her stiffened arms as if they were greased rails; she climbs the steps to her dormitory, her knees churning like pistons, and pauses before the door to stomp snow from her high, black boots; alone on a path (but Finch, hidden, watches!) she holds her books against her stomach, runs, slides like a tightwire walker on a streak of silvery ice.

Ah, thinks Finch, oblivious to his books and the dry, clean smell of the library, *beauty!* She walks and runs, this beautiful Ellen, sits, jumps, with the floating, liquid perfection of some gaudy reptile.

It was Christmas, and I was home with my family, and I had reading and research papers to do, but I—why should I not say it—was in love. Finch was eighteen, and in love for the first time in his life. Yes, *Finch loves!* Or, thought he did. Loved, once.

"Jim?" says a voice outside this absorbing, warming reality—it is his father, or his mother, come at the agreed hour. "Jim, it's time to go, we'll be late for supper." Finch opens his eyes, and it is winter again, cars make slushy noises outside the window, and he must reorder his mind, recall where he left off his research, stack his cards and papers, answer questions, think of real things, when and where and what he is.

It is Christmas Eve night, and my family gathers at the huge tree that dominates our living room. There are special things to eat, and I am allowed a little whiskey for the occasion. My mother is happy in her Christmas way, tears in her eyes as she hands me many expensive gifts, elaborately wrapped—a new fountain pen, made in Germany, with a thick barrel, so much easier for the fingers to circle; a cowhide briefcase with a manacle fitted to the handle so I can lock it to my wrist (this will require new feats of balance, but, to please her, I say nothing of it); an Astrakhan hat, in vogue among students this year—she will not have me lack what others have!

I appear to enjoy this annual ceremony as much as they. I give, and get, an enthusiastic hug and kiss as I open each gift, being careful not to too badly smash or tear the fluffy bows and ribbons and bright paper as I unwrap each package, labeled, as always, *To Jim from Santa*. I faithfully follow my father's direction as he films all this, stooped behind his camera and tripod, his words just a bit thick with too much whiskey. I pose, seated on the floor between my younger brother and sister (they are both perfectly ordinary), put my arms around their necks, do my best to smile so that I will not look drunk or half-witted in the movie.

But I go to bed early, pleading fatigue, the ritual splash of whiskey, the research to be done even on Christmas day. I leave them, to seek Ellen, to be alone in my bed and nourish this thrilling, weakening sensation of love that for the first time in my life lets me, makes me, forget myself. My taut body relaxes in stages, by degrees, while my brain whirls gently with real and imaginary visions of this exquisite Ellen. I still hear music, the rattle of happy, sentimental talk as my parents sit up late, drinking and watching old Christmas films—and for the first time in my life, I am not ashamed of the erection that keeps me from sleep.

The good doctor has just informed me that my future is limited. The paralysis, unknown to me as I labor faithfully at my schedules, as I dose myself to the point of nausea, has been progressing. Subtle as a tiny worm, my malady has eaten away at this comic body, devouring days of my life. The figures noted in my folder already record the shrinkage from atrophy. The ultimate and sure end, if progression is not arrested, will be a spasm of sufficient duration, somewhere vital, the throat, the diaphragm, and I will suffocate in a final paroxysm, no different than if I had swallowed a fishbone. Yet he asks me to speak now, reassure him that I understand and face his diagnosis calmly.

He waits, brows lifted, expectant, needing; the nurse returns my file to the cabinet drawer. I speak, for us both, a lie.

"I'm . . . not . . . alarmed," I say, almost effortlessly. True, my mouth twists in shapes wholly unrelated to the words. My tongue emerges as I finish, and I am in danger of drooling idiotically, but the words, slow-paced, are only a little distorted, like the stridency in the voices of the deaf when they sing.

True, no one could take me for normal, but that I speak at all is a minor wonder.

"Good," the doctor said, "good," washing his hands. The nurse has left the room.

I have said, does not Finch feel? But feeling brings on paralysis, interrupts the constant stream of impulses from brain to muscle—feeling means stasis, immobility. I must be alone if I am to allow myself grief or wonder. Solitude waits only on my tortured passage through the waiting room, a perilous descent of the stairs, a short ride on my bicycle to the dormitory.

Back at the university, I determined to call her. Though I might have known she would not refuse me, I shook as if I suffered Saint Vitus' dance, telephone receiver in hand, until she said yes, she would accompany me to a movie. "Will we be walking, Jimmy?" she asked. I faltered, choked, not having thought to the point of specific arrangements. Finch, pride of the history department, flustered like any juvenile! *No*, I managed to stammer: even the closest theater was a trek across the campus, far enough to be humiliating. I cringed, imagining us, arm in arm perhaps, floundering and swaying on the icy paths. "Oh," Ellen said, and waited for me to speak. I rocked fitfully on the small seat in the booth in the empty dormitory corridor. It might have sounded, in her ear, like the wild and frantic banging of someone prematurely buried.

I nearly mentioned my bicycle, but this was unsafe in winter for me alone—with her, perched on the handlebars, it would have been macabre. "I have a car, Jimmy," she said sweetly. And so we went in her car.

I do not remember what film we saw, for through most of the feature I sat rigid, inching my hand closer and closer to hers. Something happened in the film, something loud, action with bombastic musical accompaniment, and damning myself eternally a coward if I failed to act, at last, with a short, convulsive, clutching thrust, I slipped my hand over hers. She was kind enough to turn her head to me, and smile. We sat that way until the house lights came up, my sweaty palm covering the back of her smooth, cool hand. Surreptitiously, I breathed her delicious perfume, and from the corner of my eye, exulted in the delicate turn of her ear, her nostril, the way her blond hair swept upward on the back of her neck, the soft line of her throat, the faint heaving of her bosom.

We parked at the dormitory complex. It was very cold, and the other cars raised thick, steady clouds of exhaust. Their occupants, clasped in long, intense embraces, moved as shadows behind the frosted windows, all about us. Every few minutes, an engine died, a door opened, and a couple emerged to walk to one or another of the buildings. In the doorway lights we saw clearly their final kissing and fondling.

Ellen left the motor running, and we sat, silent. She wore a heavy coat, open, with a hood, a ring of snowy rabbit fur framing her face. We sat, quiet, while my brain raced, wondering what I should, or would, or could do. I did not want, at first, to touch her, but felt I must. I could feel the tic in my cheek grow worse, knew my limbs were frozen, hands balled in fists in my lap.

"Do you want me to walk with you to your dorm, Jimmy?" she said, and quickly, she leaned toward me, perhaps to open the door for me, I do not know. Somehow it terrified me, and I lurched, as if I had been given an electrical shock, and I spoke.

"No!" I said. I did not mean to touch her, not at first.

My left arm came up, swiftly enough to have given her a jarring slap, but stopped short, and I caressed her cheek and chin. She seemed to lean further toward me. I willed my right hand to take her shoulder and turn her fully toward me. I think she wanted me to kiss her, or thought I wanted to—I looked into her face, and she was, again, smiling, as she had in the theater. Her mouth was open slightly, her eyelids fluttering.

It was then I decided to kiss her, and let myself feel fully the love I had not permitted myself before, ever. I think I may have begun to cry.

I was not in love, I understand now, not in love with this beautiful Ellen, this precocious student of science, with her skin like milk, her grace of movement so inherent and unconscious as to put a dancer or an animal to shame. I did not love her, I say. I felt, then, as I moved my head closer to hers, the welling up of my response to all the love showered on me before, by my family, doctors, nurses, therapists, teachers.

Should not Finch, like you, feel?

I was, surely, crying, making a grotesque sound like the growling of a beast. I was moved by the collective force of all that love—my weepy mother, standing at the end of the parallel handrails, holding back her tears, whispering, *step Jimmy, step, one more step to mother, Jimmy*; my father, carrying me high on his shoulders in the teeth of a biting wind at a football game, cheering, *look at him go, Jimmy!*, suddenly letting me drop into his arms, hugging me to his chest, saying, *it's okay, Jim, it's okay*, because he thought I felt hurt, unable ever to run like that anonymous halfback; my teachers, *see, James knows, you're all so smart aleck, but James always has the right answer*; my sister, *Jimmy, are you the smartest person in the world?*; an auditorium filled with parents, the state superintendent of education saying, *I cannot say enough in praise of James Finch*, rolls of applause as I move, like some crippled insect, to the podium, everyone's eyes wet . . . I draw Ellen's face close to mine, my hand tightening on her shoulder. Stupidly, I try to speak.

Kiss me, I want to say, with all the force muted by all the tenderness of my need. And I am betrayed once more by my odious body. Ellen's mouth is closed to meet mine, and I gargle some ugly distortion of my intention: *Kwaryoup*, I say, and her eyes pop open in horror. I hold her tightly, feel her resistance, try again—*Keeeebryumbee*! erupts from my throat. She tries to release herself. *Sochavadeebow*, I am saying, trying to reassure her.

"Jimmy!" she says, and pulls at my wrists. "Let go, Jimmy!" I want to comply, but my left hand, nerves along my arm seeming to explode like a string of firecrackers, raises, comes down on her breast. "Jimmy!" she shrieks, and is crying now. "Get away from me, Jimmy, let go of me! Get your hands off me, you're hurting me, Jimmy!"

And it is over, mercifully. The door is open, I crawl or fall out, scramble through the snow on my hands and knees, slobbering, falling, thrashing. Behind me, I hear Ellen's nearly hysterical sobbing.

Ah, Finch, to think you might love! I no longer need to remember this, but when I do, am amused, recalling fairy tales of frogs and princesses, recited, sometimes hour after hour, in an effort to relax me for sleep, by my patient mother. A student of history, I remind myself, should have known better.

No matter. Before the following year was out, I had ceased avoiding her. When we meet now, we can even smile, though we do not speak.

As I leave, other patients in the waiting room pretend not to see me. An old woman with a cane and a platform shoe covers her eyes with a magazine. A palsied man, no more than forty, looks down at his shuddering hands. Another woman, younger, with a perfectly healthy looking child on her lap, suddenly becomes interested in her son's hair, like a grooming, lice- and salt-seeking primate. Yet another woman, her face set in a lopsided grimace, one shoulder permanently higher than the other, merely yawns, closes her eyes, pinches the bridge of her nose between two fingers until I am beyond her, as if she cannot bear her affliction so long as I am before her to remind her of it.

I walk to the door. I stagger like an old wino, head whipping from side to side with the thrust of each leg, as if I keep time to some raucous, private music. My arms are cocked, ready to catch me if I slip. My feet point inward, and my torso tips forward to provide the continuity of momentum, my broad shoulders thrown back to maintain a risky balance.

It is a gait to embarrass, to make children laugh, a clumsy cantering locomotion that results from only the most exacting and determined attention to control. Inside my rolling head, behind my shocked, magnified eyeballs, my brain orders, with utmost precision, each awkward jerk of thigh, leg, foot. Just as I reach the door to the stairs, a voice greets me cheerfully.

"Hello, Jimmy," sings out in a lilting feminine rush of genuine delight. I bang loudly against the door as I stop, gripping the knob with both hands for support. My head nearly hits the panel of thick, opaque glass. I turn with difficulty. "Hello, Jimmy," she says again.

I know her, but not well. She is a disgusting thing to see, a fellow-student. Fat of face and body, her legs are little more than pale pink, waxy skin stretched over bone, her feet strapped to the steel platform of her wheelchair. One arm is horribly withered, the thin, useless fingers held curled in her broad lap. The other is braced for strength to allow her to work the levers that steer her chair. Beneath her seat squats a large, black battery, her source of power. Her neck angles slightly to one side. Someone has recently given her jet black hair a hideous pixie cut.

I know her. She is one of the small, cohesive platoon of handicapped, crippled, maimed university students. They have an association of sorts, advised by a conscientious faculty member who lost an eye in Korea. The university provides a specially equipped Volkswagen van to take them about campus. They have keys to operate freight elevators, and the buildings have ramps to accommodate them. When I came to the university I was invited, by the one-eyed professor, to join their ranks. I even attended one meeting—mostly polio victims and amputees. The agenda was devoted to a discussion of whether or not to extend membership to an albino girl whose eyesight was so bad she could not read mimeographed class handouts. I declined to join, of course, but still receive their randomly published newsletter. We have nothing in common.

She smiles now, lipstick and powder, rouge and eyebrow pencil making a theater mask of her face. "I've never seen you up here before, Jimmy, have you just started coming?" I am struck suddenly with the awareness that she has an . . . an *interest* in me! I grope frantically to open the door.

I must, and do, speak, but badly, without thinking, so shaken am I with my understanding. *Haroyoup* comes groaning from my lips, like the creaking of a heavy casket lid. Startled and embarrassed, she smiles all the harder, and I push open the door to begin the slow descent of the steep stairs leading to the street where my bicycle waits. Mad Finch, who dared to think he might feel!

At the top of the stairs I turn around, for I must descend backwards. I take the rail with both hands, regulate my breathing, concentrate, then step back, into the air, with one foot . . . I have a special sense of freedom, for I can never know if the foot will find the stair just below, or if I will step backward into space, find nothing, and fall. I am, for an instant, like a blindfolded highdiver who steps off the springboard, uncertain if there is water below.

I am able, momentarily at least, to forget my self-pity in this kind of freedom only I know.

I must not despair! Though Finch wields the chalk no better than a child does a crayon, he cuts surely as a surgeon to the heart of the problem on the blackboard. Though his pronunciation is atrocious, his syntax is exact, his structure flawless, vocabulary well beyond his years. Though his eyes, enlarged behind thick lenses, stare, sometimes roll up in his head, no one reads more or faster, and for amusement he will commit a paragraph or a page to memory in record time.

It is Finch who is free to traverse the lines of caste and class in our community. Finch is the locker room pet of brainless athletes. They challenge him to feats of strength, and lose goodnaturedly. From the heights of their chickenwire and toilet paper float thrones, Junoesque sorority queens wave to Finch in the crowd, call him by name. Filthy and morose, the bearded politicals and bohemians, who lurk in the basement of the student union, will take time to read Finch their latest throwaway or poem. Serious students, praying for futures in government or academia, consult Finch before submitting seminar reports.

Oh, I am not lonely!

So, with an effort of will, informed by the discipline of my regimen in physical therapy, weightlifting, my schedules, I heave, lifting my center of balance upward with an exaggerated shrug of my broad, strong shoulders; then, at the exact moment, a second divided into several parts for precision, I lean to the right, forcing all my weight onto my right leg, onto the raised pedal of my bicycle. There is no continuity, no fluid evolving process of motion, but my timing is correct—my mind has once more concentrated this fool's body into a preconceived pattern—the pedal depresses, the bike rolls forward.

There is an instant when disaster is possible—I am thrown forward with the bike, but my locked left hand grips the handlebar, stops me short of an ignominious and bruising tumble to the pavement. I remember to pull with my right arm, to isolate the individual muscles that will steer out, away from the curb, past the hulk of a parked florist's truck.

I move. Out now, near the center line, I assert the series of stiff, dramatic thrusts of hip and leg that pump me along, past the campus shops, the bus stop.

Students throng the sidewalk, and they call to me. The frat boys, the unmercifully attractive girls, golden and creamy in their expensive clothes, jocks in their letter sweaters and windbreakers, malcontents in old military jackets. They call: "Ho Finch!" "Jimbo!" "Hi Jimmy!" They grin, wave. "Baby Jim boy!" "Hi Jim," they call.

With careful, paced breathing, I multiply the complexity of my ordeal. Almost one by one, I unlock my fingers from the handlebar. With the strained deliberation of a weightlifter, I raise it above my head, steering and balance both entrusted to my left arm. Aloft, the tingling spasms are sufficient to produce a casual wave. Like a swimmer shaking water from his inner ear, I rock my head, once, twice, three times, until I face them. Opening my jaw is enough to pull my lips back over my teeth: a smile.

In this instant I am helpless. Were a car to swerve into my path, a pedestrian dart in front of me, all would end in an absurd, theatrical collision—perhaps serious injury. But I prevail.

Now, the breeze in my ears, my glasses vibrating on the bridge of my nose, threatening to fall across my mouth, I speak. My tongue bucks and floats, the stiff planes of my throat shiver, and I respond.

"Jimmy!" they cry. "How you doing, Jimbo!"

Hyaroul explodes my voice, and I can almost see their delight, the fullness of quick and easy tears of sentimental pity form in their eyes. *Hyarouffa*! I say, already plotting how I will lower my right hand, face the road again. *Haluff*! I make of unexpelled breath, not knowing if it is my cry of joy at being alive, known, loved, or a curse far more terrible than any profane cliché they will ever know—because . . . I suspect . . . simply because I cannot answer my own questions, cannot know what is, or is not, Finch.

In Body, a Passenger, and Rumpled

"The witness of the body," to use Delmore Schwartz's telling phrase, is keenly felt by the handicapped. Ben Belitt, seeing the marred face of a charwoman at four in the morning, is suddenly made partner to this awareness. The same poet in "Veteran's Hospital" shows us men bound to their bodies by the apparatus of disability. The blind poet Felix Pollak shows how blindness, the diminishing of a part of the body, makes it more present. Stuttering enhances the appreciation of perfect speech as Alan Dugan's poem spells out. The solicitous attitude of overhelpful friends makes Harold Bond yet more aware of his body as he shows in the good-natured irony of his poem "The Game." Christopher Fahy's poem "The Stroke" shows the body as an inescapable prison. But it is left to the elegant verses of Richard Wilbur to sing that the disabled share the mystery and dignity of incarnate beings.

Charwoman

(Lower Manhattan—6:00 P.M.)

Clapping the door to, in the little light,
In the stair-fall's deepening plunge,
I see, in the slate dark, the lumped form, like a sponge,
Striking a rote erasure in the night—

And keep that figure; while a watery arc
Trembles and wanes in wetted tile, as if
It wrote all darkness down in hieroglyph
And spoke vendetta with a water-mark.

That shadowy flare shall presently define
A scuffed and hazardous wrist, a ruined jaw
Packed into goitre, like a pigeon's craw,
A bitten elbow webbed with a naphtha line;

While light shall lessen, blunting, by brute degrees,
The world's waste scanted to a personal sin,
Till all is darkness where her brush has been
And blinds the blackening marble by her knees.

*   *   *

I mark what way the dropping shaft-light went;
It flung the day's drowned faces out, and fell
Hasped like a coffin down a darkening well:
And poise on the shaft-way for my own descent.

Reprinted by permission of the author from *New and Selected Poems*; copyright © by Ben Belitt.

Veteran's Hospital
(White River Junction, Vt.)

Bringing "only what is needed—essential
toilet articles" in a paper bag,
dressed as for dying, one sees the dying plainly.
These are the homecomings of Agamemnon,
the voyages to the underside of the web
that weaves and unweaves while the suitors gorge upon plenty
and the languishing sons at home unwish their warring
fathers, with strong electric fingers.
The fathers are failing.
In the Hospital Exchange, one sees the dying plainly:
color televisions, beach towels, automatic razors—
the hardware of the affluent society marked
down to cost, to match the negative afflatus
of the ailing, the bandages and badges of their status.
Under the sand-bags, rubber hoses, pipettes, bed-clamps,
tax-exempt, amenable as rabbits,
the unenlisted men are bleeding through their noses
in a perimeter of ramps and apparatus.

In that prosthetic world, the Solarium
lights a junkpile of used parts: the hip that caught
a ricochet of shrapnel; tattoos in curing meats;
scars like fizzled fuses; cancelled postage stamps;
automated claws in candy; the Laser's edge; and barium.
The nurses pass like mowers, dressing and
undressing in the razor-sharp incisions
and the flowering phosphorescence. The smell
of rubbing alcohol rises on desertions and deprivals
and divorces. It is incorruptible. A wheelchair aims
its hospital pajamas like a gun-emplacement.
The amputee is swinging in his aviary.
His fingers walk the bird-bars.
There is singing
from the Ward-Room—a buzzing of transistors
like blueflies in a urinal. War over war,
the expendables of Metz and Château-Thierry,

the guerillas of Bien-Hoa and Korea,
the draftees, the Reserves, the re-enlisters,
open a common wave-length. The catatonic
sons are revving up their combos in the era
of the angry adolescent: their cry is electronic.
Their thumbs are armed with picks. The acid-rock guitarist
in metals studs and chevrons, bombed with magnesium,
mourns like a country yokel, and the innocents
are slaughtered.

        On the terrace, there are juices
and bananas. The convalescent listens to his
heart-beat. The chaplain and his non-combative daughter
smile by the clubbed plants on the portico.

                        They shall overcome.

Visit to the Institute for the Blind

I. *The Walk*

Swimming against the coarse grain
of sun-streaked air, I am intercepted
by the crisscross of fins, the sparkle
of black diamond scales and the greetings
of strangers of long standing, who slip
their arms under mine, steering me like a
shipwreck. *Watch out!* they cry, *there's
a step!*, and heave me off my feet so that I
stumble and slip, leaving my arm behind.
When they finally leave me and dissolve
into fibres of mist, my thankyous damn
their eyes.

II. *The Institute*

All objects have evaporated here, turned into
sounds and echoes. Walls are white vibrations
nesting on fingertips, doors are brown currents
of space. The lounge is traversed by whispers
in various keys of blackness, with occasional
glints and flickers under closed lids—
memories stalking the scents of rows upon rows
of roses. The hum of stirred-up bees inside the
soft-drink automat: all the black spectacles turn
towards it—opaque shades drawn over milky windows:
Eyes are an endangered species here, grapes into
raisins.

In a corner, a woman stretches the feelers of her
private night across a page, caressing meaning.
A young man, chin on his chest (contemplating existence?),
suddenly rises and begins to pace the floor,
in a time-charted curved line, avoiding the reverberations
of shadows. Wherever he moves is the dark side
of the moon.

III. *The Dream*

That night, I dreamed of quicksand.
There was no longer any pain in sinking,
now that my fear of drowning was
drowning with me. It was the anti-climax
of a firstnight, after too many
dress rehearsals.

Stutterer

Courage: your tongue has left
its natural position in the cheek
where eddies of the breath
are navigable calms. Now
it locks against the glottis or
is snapped at by the teeth
in mid stream: it must be work
to get out what you mean:
the rapids of the breath
are furious with belief
and want the tongue, as blood
and animal of speech,
to stop it, block it, or come clean
over the rocks of teeth
and down the races of the air,
tumbled and bruised to death.
Relax it into acting, be
the air's straw-hat
canoeist with a mandolin
yodelling over the falls.
This is the sound advice
of experts and a true despair:
it is the toll to pass the locks
down to the old mill stream
where lies of love are fair.

The Game

You are my friends. You do things
for me. My affliction is
your hangup. It is yours more
than it ever could be mine.
You spread my affliction thin

enough to go around once
for all of us. You put my
coat on for me when I ask
you. You put my coat on for
me when I do not ask you.

You embrace my shoes with your
compassion. You tell me I
would be less apt to fall with
rubber soles. You carry things
for me. You tell me they are

heavy things, how it would be
difficult for anyone
to carry them. You open
mustard bottles for me. You
tell me how hard it is to

open mustard bottles. I
agree with you. I will not
destroy our game. At night I
dream I am Samson. I will
topple coliseums. I

will overwhelm you with my
brute power. I will knock you
dead. I will open mustard
bottles for you. I will show
you how easy it really is.

Originally published in *The Young American Poets* (Follet/Big Table Books, 1968) and reprinted with permission from *Dancing on Water* (The Cummington Press, 1970); copyright © by Harold Bond.

The Stroke

attacks while he's on the toilet,
thin dull pain and yellow stars.
The bright world dies.

His new self wakes contracted
dry.
He starts again
can't finish.

His numbness struggles
with oatmeal, loses to
his once fastidious chin.
Words are boulders
that roll on his tongue,
burst.

Gray shadows of family
gather
in too loud blurred TV.
Decisions
hang in the closet,
time rusts shut.

He dozes with half a world
in each eye
waits with animal cries
on the collar of hope.

His blazing pride
his fractured will
his vanity
can't thaw his frozen wrist.

The Eye (Part II)

". . . all this beastly seeing"
    —D. H. Lawrence

FOR JOHN AND BILL

I. One morning in St. Thomas, when I tried
   Our host's binoculars, what was magnified?
   In the green slopes about us, only green,
   Brisked into fronds and paddles, could be seen,
   Till by a lunging focus I was shown
   Some portion of a terrace like our own.
   Someone with ankles crossed, in tennis shoes,
   Was turning sun-blank pages of the news,
   To whom in time came espadrilles of pink
   Bearing a tall and fruit-crowned tropic drink.
   How long I witnessed, missing not a sip!—
   Then, scanning down through photons to a ship
   In the blue bay, spelt out along the bow
   The queenly legend of her name; and now
   Followed her shuttling lighter as it bore
   Her jounced, gay charges landward to explore
   Charlotte Amalie, with its duty-free
   Leicas, binoculars, and jewelry.
   What kept me goggling all that hour? The nice
   Discernment of a lime or lemon slice?
   A hope of lewd espials? An astounded
   Sense of the import of a thing surrounded—
   Of what a Z or almond-leaf became
   Within the sudden premise of a frame?
   All these, and that my eye should flutter there,
   By shrewd promotion, in the outstretched air,
   An unseen genius of the middle distance,
   Giddy with godhead or with nonexistence.

II. Preserve us, Lucy,
    From the eye's nonsense, you by whom
    Benighted Dante was beheld,
    To whom he was beholden.

If the salesman's head
Rolls on the seat-back of the 'bus
In ugly sleep, his open mouth
Banjo-strung with spittle,

Forbid my vision
To take itself for a curious angel.
Remind me that I am here in body,
A passenger, and rumpled.

Charge me to see
In all bodies the beat of spirit,
Not merely in the *tout en l'air*
Or double pike with layout

But in the strong,
Shouldering gait of the legless man,
The calm walk of the blind young woman
Whose cane touches the curbstone.

Correct my view
That the far mountain is much diminished,
That the fovea is prime composer,
That the lid's closure frees me.

Let me be touched
By the alien hands of love forever,
That this eye not be folly's loophole
But giver of due regard.

Beam in the Eye

Society often has a "beam in the eye" when it views those of its members who are less than perfect physical specimens. Death is frequently the easiest solution, as in Miller Williams' poem "The Ones That Are Thrown Out." A mother sees no other way to cope with her retarded son than to institutionalize him in Ann Tyler's short story "Average Waves in Unprotected Waters." In Natalie Petesch's story "The Street," the deformed beggar is jeered at finally by the prostitute, though he has the bitter satisfaction of getting a better spot from which to beg because for a few times he has bought Le Sylphe. Finding he can hold down a rewarding job gives a boy with dyslexia a feeling of self-worth but subtly separates him from his adored brother in James Corpora's story. In David Keller's poem "Silences," a stutterer's "silences" are more welcome than his words. "The Glen" by Josephine Jacobsen shows us a woman hoping that her young retarded stepdaughter will find and eat the poisoned mushroom. Finally, the brilliant and terrible gem from Fergus Reid Buckley is the story of ignorant peasants who in contempt make a spastic the fool in the village carnival. The boy brings off his part well, but the conclusion is grim.

The Ones That Are Thrown Out

One has flippers. This one is like a seal.
One has gills. This one is like a fish.
One has webbed hands, is like a duck.
One has a little tail, is like a pig.
One is like a frog
with no dome at all above the eyes.

They call them bad babies.

They didn't mean to be bad
but who does.

Reprinted by permission of Louisiana State University Press from *Distractions* by Miller Williams;
copyright © 1979.

Average Waves in Unprotected Waters

As soon as it got light, Bet woke him and dressed him, and then she walked him over to the table and tried to make him eat a little cereal. He wouldn't, though. He could tell something was up. She pressed the edge of the spoon against his lips till she heard it click on his teeth, but he just looked off at a corner of the ceiling—a knobby child with great glassy eyes and her own fair hair. Like any other nine-year-old, he wore a striped shirt and jeans, but the shirt was too neat and the jeans too blue, un-patched and unfaded, and would stay that way till he outgrew them. And his face was elderly—pinched, strained, tired—though it should have looked as unused as his jeans. He hardly ever changed his expression.

She left him in his chair and went to make the beds. Then she raised the yellowed shade, rinsed a few spoons in the bathroom sink, picked up some bits of magazines he'd torn the night before. This was a rented room in an ancient, crumbling house, and nothing you could do to it would lighten its cluttered look. There was always that feeling of too many lives layered over other lives, like the layers of brownish wallpaper her child had peeled away in the corner by his bed.

She slipped her feet into flat-heeled loafers and absently patted the front of her dress, a worn beige knit she usually saved for Sundays. Maybe she should take it in a little; it hung from her shoulders like a sack. She felt too slight and frail, too wispy for all she had to do today. But she reached for her coat anyhow, and put it on and tied a blue kerchief under her chin. Then she went over to the table and slowly spun, modelling the coat. "See, Arnold?" she said. "We're going out."

Arnold went on looking at the ceiling, but his gaze turned wild and she knew he'd heard.

She fetched his jacket from the closet—brown corduroy, with a hood. It had set her back half a week's salary. But Arnold didn't like it; he always wanted his old one, a little red duffel coat he'd long ago outgrew. When she came toward him, he started moaning and rocking and shaking his head. She had to struggle to stuff his arms in the sleeves. Small though he was, he was strong, wiry; he was getting to be too much for her. He shook free of her hands and ran over to his bed. The jacket was on, though. It wasn't buttoned, the collar was askew, but never mind; that just made him look more real. She always felt bad at how he stood inside his clothes, separate from them, passive, unaware of all the buttons and snaps she'd fastened as carefully as she would a doll's.

She gave a last look around the room, checked to make sure the hot plate was off, and then picked up her purse and Arnold's suitcase. "Come along, Arnold," she said.

He came, dragging out every step. He looked at the suitcase suspiciously, but only because it was new. It didn't have any meaning for him. "See?" she said. "It's yours. It's Arnold's. It's going on the train with us."

But her voice was all wrong. He would pick it up, for sure. She paused in the middle of locking the door and glanced over at him fearfully. Anything could set him off nowadays. He hadn't noticed, though. He was too busy staring around the hallway, goggling at a freckled, walnut-framed mirror as if he'd never seen it before. She touched his shoulder. "Come, Arnold," she said.

They went down the stairs slowly, both of them clinging to the sticky mahogany railing. The suitcase banged against her shins. In the entrance hall, old Mrs. Puckett stood waiting outside her door—a huge, soft lady in a black crêpe dress and orthopedic shoes. She was holding a plastic bag of peanut-butter cookies, Arnold's favorites. There were tears in her eyes. "Here, Arnold," she said, quavering. Maybe she felt to blame that he was going. But she'd done the best she could: baby-sat him all these years and only given up when he'd grown too strong and wild to manage. Bet wished Arnold would give the old lady some sign—hug her, make his little crowing noise, just take the cookies, even. But he was too excited. He raced on out the front door, and it was Bet who had to take them. "Well, thank you, Mrs. Puckett," she said. "I know he'll enjoy them later."

"Oh, no . . ." said Mrs. Puckett, and she flapped her large hands and gave up, sobbing.

They were lucky and caught a bus first thing. Arnold sat by the window. He must have thought he was going to work with her; when they passed the red-and-gold Kresge's sign, he jabbered and tried to stand up. "No, honey," she said, and took hold of his arm. He settled down then and let his hand stay curled in hers awhile. He had very small, cool fingers, and nails as smooth as thumbtack heads.

At the train station, she bought the tickets and then a pack of Wrigley's spearmint gum. Arnold stood gaping at the vaulted ceiling, with his head flopped back and his arms hanging limp at his sides. People stared at him. She would have liked to push their faces in. "Over here, honey," she said, and she nudged him toward the gate, straightening his collar as they walked.

He hadn't been on a train before and acted a little nervous, bouncing up and down in his seat and flipping the lid of his ashtray and craning forward to see the man ahead of them. When the train started moving, he crowed and pulled at her sleeve. "That's right, Arnold. Train. We're taking a trip," Bet said. She unwrapped a stick of chewing gum and gave it to him. He loved gum. If she didn't watch him closely, he sometimes swallowed it—which worried her a little because she'd heard it clogged your kidneys; but at least it would keep him busy. She looked down at the top of his head. Through the blond prickles of his hair, cut short for practical reasons, she could see his skull bones moving as he chewed. He was so thin-skinned, almost transparent; sometimes she imagined she could see the blood travelling in his veins.

When the train reached a steady speed, he grew calmer, and after a while he nodded over against her and let his hands sag on his knees. She watched his eyelashes slowly drooping—two colorless, fringed crescents, heavier and heavier, every now and then flying up as he tried to fight off sleep. He had never slept well, not ever, not even as a baby. Even before they'd noticed anything wrong, they'd wondered at his jittery, jerky catnaps, his tiny hands clutching tight and springing open, his strange single wail sailing out while he went right on sleeping. Avery said it gave him the chills. And after the doctor talked to them Avery wouldn't have anything to do with Arnold anymore—just walked in wide circles around the crib, looking stunned and sick. A few weeks later, he left. She wasn't surprised. She even knew how he felt, more or less. Halfway, he blamed her; halfway, he blamed himself. You can't believe a thing like this will just fall on you out of nowhere.

She'd had moments herself of picturing some kind of evil gene in her husband's ordinary stocky body—a dark little egg like a black jelly bean, she imagined it. All his fault. But other times she was sure the gene was hers. It seemed so natural; she never could do anything as well as most people. And then other times she blamed their marriage. They'd married too young, against her parents' wishes. All she'd wanted was to get away from home. Now she couldn't remember why. What was wrong with home? She thought of her parents' humped green trailer, perched on cinder blocks near a forest of masts in Salt Spray, Maryland. At this distance (parents dead, trailer rusted to bits, even Salt Spray changed past recognition), it seemed to her that her old life had been beautifully free and spacious. She closed her eyes and saw wide gray skies. Everything had been ruled by the sea. Her father (who'd run a fishing boat for tourists) couldn't arrange his day till he'd heard the marine forecast—the wind, the tides, the smallcraft warnings, the height of average waves in unprotected waters. He loved to fish, offshore and on, and he swam every chance he could get. He'd tried to teach her to bodysurf, but it hadn't worked out. There was something about the breakers: she just gritted her teeth and stood staunch and let them slam into her. As if standing staunch were a virtue, really. She couldn't explain it. Her father thought she was scared, but it wasn't that at all.

She'd married Avery against their wishes and been sorry ever since—

sorry to move so far from home, sorrier when her parents died within a year of each other, sorriest of all when the marriage turned grim and cranky. But she never would have thought of leaving him. It was Avery who left; she would have stayed forever. In fact, she did stay on in their apartment for months after he'd gone, though the rent was far too high. It wasn't that she expected him back. She just took some comfort from enduring.

Arnold's head snapped up. He looked around him and made a gurgling sound. His chewing gum fell onto the front of his jacket. "Here, honey," she told him. She put the gum in her ashtray. "Look out the window. See the cows?"

He wouldn't look. He began bouncing in his seat, rubbing his hands together rapidly.

"Arnold? Want a cookie?"

If only she'd brought a picture book. She'd meant to and then forgot. She wondered if the train people sold magazines. If she let him get too bored, he'd go into one of his tantrums, and then she wouldn't be able to handle him. The doctor had given her pills just in case, but she was always afraid that while he was screaming he would choke on them. She looked around the car. "Arnold," she said, "see the . . . see the hat with feathers on? Isn't it pretty? See the red suitcase? See the, um . . ."

The car door opened with a rush of clattering wheels and the conductor burst in, singing "Girl of my dreams, I love you." He lurched down the aisle, plucking pink tickets from the back of each seat. Just across from Bet and Arnold, he stopped. He was looking down at a tiny black lady in a purple coat, with a fox fur piece biting its own tail around her neck. "You!" he said.

The lady stared straight ahead.

"You, I saw you. You're the one in the washroom."

A little muscle twitched in her cheek.

"You got on this train in Beulah, didn't you. Snuck in the washroom. Darted back like you thought you could put something over on me. I saw that bit of purple! Where's your ticket gone to?"

She started fumbling in a blue cloth purse. The fumbling went on and on. The conductor shifted his weight.

"Why!" she said finally. "I must've left it back in my other seat."

"What other seat?"

"Oh, the one back . . ." She waved a spidery hand.

The conductor sighed. "Lady," he said, "you owe me money."

"I do no such thing!" she said. "Viper! Monger! Hitler!" Her voice screeched up all at once; she sounded like a parrot. Bet winced and felt herself flushing, as if *she* were the one. But then at her shoulder she heard a sudden, rusty clang, and she turned and saw that Arnold was laughing.

He had his mouth wide open and his tongue curled, the way he did when he watched "Sesame Street." Even after the scene had worn itself out, and the lady had paid and the conductor had moved on, Arnold went on chortling and la-la-ing, and Bet looked gratefully at the little black lady, who was settling her fur piece and muttering under her breath.

From the Parkinsville Railroad Station, which they seemed to be tearing down or else remodelling—she couldn't tell which—they took a taxicab to Parkins State Hospital. "Oh, I been out there many and many a time," said the driver. "Went out there just the other——"

But she couldn't stop herself; she had to tell him before she forgot. "Listen," she said, "I want you to wait for me right in the driveway. I don't want you to go on away."

"Well, fine," he said.

"Can you do that? I want you to be sitting right by the porch or the steps or whatever, right where I come out of, ready to take me back to the station. Don't just go off and——"

"I *got* you, I got you," he said.

She sank back. She hoped he understood.

Arnold wanted a peanut-butter cookie. He was reaching and whimpering. She didn't know what to do. She wanted to give him anything he asked for, anything; but he'd get it all over his face and arrive not looking his best. She couldn't stand it if they thought he was just ordinary and unattractive. She wanted them to see how small and neat he was, how somebody cherished him. But it would be awful if he went into one of his rages. She broke off a little piece of cookie from the bag. "Here," she told him. "Don't mess, now."

He flung himself back in the corner and ate it, keeping one hand flattened across his mouth while he chewed.

The hospital looked like someone's great pillared mansion, with square brick buildings all around it. "Here we are," the driver said.

"Thank you," she said. "Now you wait here, please. Just wait till I get——"

"*Lady*," he said. "I'll wait."

She opened the door and nudged Arnold out ahead of her. Lugging the suitcase, she started toward the steps. "Come on, Arnold," she said.

He hung back.

"Arnold?"

Maybe he wouldn't allow it, and they would go on home and never think of this again.

But he came, finally, climbing the steps in his little hobbled way. His face was clean, but there were a few cookie crumbs on his jacket. She set down the suitcase to brush them off. Then she buttoned all his buttons and smoothed his shirt collar over his jacket collar before she pushed open the door.

In the admitting office, a lady behind a wooden counter showed her what papers to sign. Secretaries were clacketing typewriters all around. Bet thought Arnold might like that, but instead he got lost in the lights—chilly, hanging ice-cube tray lights with a little flicker to them. He gazed upward, looking astonished. Finally a flat-fronted nurse came in and touched his elbow. "Come along, Arnold. Come, Mommy. We'll show you where Arnold is staying," she said.

They walked back across the entrance hall, then up wide marble steps with hollows worn in them. Arnold clung to the bannister. There was a smell Bet hated, pine-oil disinfectant, but Arnold didn't seem to notice. You never knew; sometimes smells could just put him in a state.

The nurse unlocked a double door that had chicken-wired windows. They walked through a corridor, passing several fat, ugly women in shapeless gray dresses and ankle socks. "Ha!" one of the women said, and fell giggling into the arms of a friend. The nurse said, "*Here* we are." She led them into an enormous hallway lined with little white cots. Nobody else was in it; there wasn't a sign that children lived here except for a tiny cardboard clown picture hanging on one vacant wall. "This one is your bed, Arnold," said the nurse. Bet laid the suitcase on it. It was made up so neatly, the sheets might have been painted on. A steely-gray blanket was folded across the foot. She looked over at Arnold, but he was pivoting back and forth to hear how his new sneakers squeaked on the linoleum.

"Usually," said the nurse, "we like to give new residents six months before the family visits. That way they settle in quicker, don't you see." She turned away and adjusted the clown picture, though as far as Bet could tell it was fine the way it was. Over her shoulder, the nurse said, "You can tell him goodbye now, if you like."

"Oh," Bet said. "All right." She set her hands on Arnold's shoulders. Then she laid her face against his hair, which felt warm and fuzzy. "Honey," she said. But he went on pivoting. She straightened and told the nurse, "I brought his special blanket."

"Oh, fine," said the nurse, turning toward her again. "We'll see that he gets it."

"He always likes to sleep with it; he has ever since he was little."

"All right."

"Don't wash it. He hates if you wash it."

"Yes. Say goodbye to Mommy now, Arnold."

"A lot of times he'll surprise you. I mean there's a whole lot to him. He's not just——"

"We'll take very good care of him, Mrs. Blevins, don't worry."

"Well," she said. "'Bye, Arnold."

She left the ward with the nurse and went down the corridor. As the nurse was unlocking the doors for her, she heard a single, terrible scream, but the nurse only patted her shoulder and pushed her gently on through.

In the taxi, Bet said, "Now, I've just got fifteen minutes to get to the station. I wonder if you could hurry?"

"Sure thing," the driver said.

She folded her hands and looked straight ahead. Tears seemed to be coming down her face in sheets.

Once she'd reached the station, she went to the ticket window. "Am I in time for the twelve-thirty-two?" she asked.

"Easily," said the man. "It's twenty minutes late."

"What?"

"Got held up in Norton somehow."

"But you can't!" she said. The man looked startled. She must be a sight, all swollen-eyed and wet-cheeked. "Look," she said, in a lower voice. "I figured this on purpose. I chose the one train from Beulah that would let me catch another one back without waiting. I do not want to sit and wait in this station."

"Twenty *minutes*, lady. That's all it is."

"What am I going to do?" she asked him.

He turned back to his ledgers.

She went over to a bench and sat down. Ladders and scaffolding towered above her, and only ten or twelve passengers were dotted through the rest of the station. The place looked bombed out—nothing but a shell. "Twenty minutes!" she said aloud. "What am I going to do?"

Through the double glass doors at the far end of the station, a procession of gray-suited men arrived with briefcases. More men came behind them, dressed in work clothes, carrying folding chairs, black trunklike boxes with silver hinges, microphones, a wooden lectern, and an armload of bunting. They set the lectern down in the center of the floor, not six feet from Bet. They draped the bunting across it—an arc of red, white, and blue. Wires were connected, floodlights were lit. A microphone screeched. One of the workmen said, "Try her, Mayor." He held the microphone out to a fat man in a suit, who cleared his throat and said, "Ladies and gentlemen, on the occasion of the expansion of this fine old railway station——"

"Sure do get an echo here," the workman said. "Keep on going."

The Mayor cleared his throat again. "If I may," he said, "I'd like to take about twenty minutes of your time, friends."

He straightened his tie. Bet blew her nose, and then she wiped her eyes and smiled. They had come just for her sake, you might think. They were putting on a sort of private play. From now on, all the world was going to be like that—just something on a stage, for her to sit back and watch.

The Street

The tourists think I'm some kind of idiot, but I'm not. I understand everything they say, about me and about other things in the Quarter. Sometimes on a sunny afternoon on Bourbon Street their laughter will carry from across the street where they are standing in front of Marty's sign: Five Beautiful Girls—A Show Every Hour. (They're not all beautiful. Only La Sylphe.)

I can always tell when the tourists are no longer looking at the girls' pictures but are looking across the street where I am; their laughter stops, there is a sudden silence. That is when I know they are looking at me.

Usually I take my place in the street across from Marty's Place about dark. Sundays across from St. Louis' Church is not a bad place either, but in Jackson Square you have to compete with the artists; on Bourbon Street I only have to compete with Duke. He taps. Sometimes he picks up so much coin he can't go on tapping, else it falls out of his pockets. The tourists like to throw small coins like confetti, and they like to see the Duke pick it up. It's like they've been down on their knees all their lives making it, and now they can say: "Here, see what it's like." When the Duke gets too much coin in his pockets, he pretends he wants a beer and goes in the Red Barn where the bartender knows him. The Duke gives him a tip and, there in the back where nobody can see him, they turn the coin into folding money. That is one way. Every street beggar has his way of turning coin into bills. My way is different.

Everybody likes laughing at the Duke; he acts old-timey, like Hip Williams in Les Caves. He sings real nigger-style, a kind of hopped-up Fats Waller. He makes a mint, that Hip. And Duke and Hip, sometimes they do a team. They go right up Bourbon, down Royal and back through Chartres, tapping, singing and tambourining, like slavery was the latest invention of the tourists. Daytimes, they go to Tulane.

I started to go to Tulane myself once because I wanted to get off the Street. That was before I started saving my money. But I've only got one hand that's good and it's rough getting up the steps, especially without a ramp. You've got to have somebody to push you everywhere. One time the kid who was supposed to push me didn't show up, and I sat there in the snow a whole hour. I was covered with it, there was no one in the street to get me up the steps. I had pneumonia two weeks that time, and after that I came back to the Street. If you make enough money you can get off. That is the only way.

Reprinted by permission of the author from *Snapdragon*, Spring 1982; copyright © by Natalie Petesch.

My place on Bourbon Street is a good one. I give Hawaii Jim half my take and he lets me stay in front of his place. If I get a bill I can tuck it away in my underclothes, but coins are harder; they jingle, and when around four A.M. they pick me up from the sidewalk and put me in my chair, the money will fall out sometimes. Hawaii gets mad at me then. He'll throw the money at me and yell, "For cryin out loud, if you're gonna be a thief, why don't you get in the big time?" It seems on those mornings when they catch me with extra dimes or quarters they always have trouble getting me into my chair.

My problem with the chair is a special one, and they know it. When I'm down on the sidewalk, it's O.K. The fact that both legs are twisted in opposite directions gives me a kind of balance. I mean, that way I am pretty solid on the ground with the weight on my thighs—Duncan Phyfe they call me. My left arm is good for resting on too; it doesn't bend, but holds me up straight as a post on the sidewalk. By some odd coincidence, when it formed, the palm curled cuplike. This gives me a big advantage with the tourists.

Why they think I'm an idiot is because of the "major bone deformation." It kept the jawbone from growing and, later, when the teeth came in, there was no room for them; so the mouth won't shut and that makes the jaw look slack. They gave my mother free powdered milk, and cornmeal and lard. There was no Vitamin D, they told her later, in the milk. She worked in a laundry nights, and slept days and we didn't get any sunlight, so it is only rickets, not polio. That was thirty years ago. Now they put things in, even in those CARE packages, so nobody has rickets anymore.

Truth is stranger than fiction. I heard once that a mother let her baby starve even while it was sucking the blood from her breasts. She didn't know the baby wasn't gaining weight. That was a long time ago in my grandmother's time, and nobody is that ignorant anymore. But the baby died anyway.

I have powerful hearing though, and I wear strong glasses so I don't miss a thing on the Street. The right eye slips, what they call walleye, and that makes me look funny. Years ago when I got my full growth, an operation might have straightened it out. The optic nerve it is. But at that time I'd really just begun saving my money. Because I wanted to get off the Street. I thought, if you save enough money, you will be free. If you have money, you can buy anything. People will shake your hand even if it feels like driftwood. So until La Sylphe showed up at Marty's Place about two months ago, it was like I'd been thinking of just one thing all my life: how to get off the Street. Then when La Sylphe started doing her act, I found that the Street could give you a bitter kind of pleasure. I mean if you cannot have the one thing you want, some other thing—like a woman—can make you stop wanting it, at least for a while. That is why I began thinking of money not only as a way to get off the Street, but as a way, just once, to get La Sylphe. I tried to increase my take. I even began to wear dark glasses and clothes that did not match, like I could not see what to put on. That picked up business a lot. It is funny but if a tourist thinks you cannot see, he thinks you cannot hear either. I have heard strange things from tourists on the Street.

But if you want to know how I really feel about tourists, I'll tell you. I hate them. They've got feet and still they walk all over you. They stumble over me where I sit on the sidewalk, and I can't get out of their way. They walk around drinking "pinkies" from those Pat O'Brien hurricane glasses, and the first thing I know they're in my lap, glasses and all. When they break one of those glasses, I have to sit in the splinters all night, the sidewalks are always too crowded to hose down at night. It's the tourists who dirty up the Street so we have to have a law in the Quarter for the residents to clean their sidewalks every day . . . gum wrappers, straws, cigars, napkins, Kodak film, rotting flowers—whatever falls from them they drop in my street. But in the morning, when they go back to their hotels, the beautiful colors of the Vieux Carré come out again, like after a rainy night, the rainbow.

Then the children come out to go to school. They come by in maroon-colored uniforms and knee socks and file by me to the nuns' school. Some are scared of me and cross over to the other side of the street when they see me. But Amélie Godchaux is my friend. She taught me to play piano with one hand. That is the thing in life I like best to do. One day I pushed my wheel into the Old Slave Patio; they had a piano there, waiting to be moved. Amy taught me F A C E. Then she taught me to play something by Joseph Haydn. It was simple and I liked it, and Amy cried. I asked her why she cried, and she said it was because I played the notes so beautifully. In my room, though, there isn't enough space for a piano. So what I wanted was to get an accordion. An accordion is different. You can peg one side without needing to bend your fingers much, and my right hand really is strong. If you lifted me to a bar at the gym I could hang my whole weight on it. I can rest my weight on my arm and not even tremble. So I could probably learn to play an accordion real good. There are places where people sing and play the accordion. They don't pass the hat, either, but get paid a regular salary, like bank clerks.

Amy would have liked that. I know she did not like me to sit in the street, especially when it rained. Sometimes she would save out something for me from her lunch box and give it to me on her way from school. I did not want it—I am never hungry—but I took it to please Amy. She would smile. She had small white teeth, like they were baby teeth, but they weren't; she was older than that, though still a child.

That was the trouble. Amy was good, but she was only a child. No body yet. I mean she did not suffer from it yet. She could never have guessed what I suffered because of La Sylphe. While Amy was asleep, dreaming of dancing lessons, I would be watching La Sylphe from where I squatted on the sidewalk, knowing I would die if I never had a girl like La Sylphe.

Between the two girls, there was probably not ten years difference— years like a lifetime. Listening to Amy in her white knee socks and parochial school uniform as she chattered about *ma mère, mon père et ma petite soeur Lisette*, was like being in Church. Watching La Sylphe was like being in hell. Yet both gave me pleasure—I did not want to give up either.

La Sylphe was the best stripper Marty ever had. She came from Nebraska, she never said what town. She told me later this was her first job, and that the other girls hated her because she was young. When the harvest was in, she told me, she and her father used to sit around and watch TV shows 'til early morning. One night her father seduced her. When the men on the next farm found it out, they used it against her, to make her give in, or else they'd tell the school principal, they said. Of course they told anyway. The mother had run away long ago with another man.

That is the way they all start on the Street. First cornfields and love, then the slow rot. But La Sylphe was a long way from rotting when I met her. She told me she had been working at Marty's only a month, when she first talked to me. That was about Easter time.

I could always see her plain as day from where I sat in the Street because Marty kept his doors open, just like they all do in the Quarter, so the tourists will gape at the girls. Then Marty would shame them. He'd say: "A new show every hour. No minimum, no cover. But don't stand in the doorway like that. Only bums do that." So then they would come in and pay two bucks for a six-ounce beer. And you had to drink up, you couldn't just sip it.

Marty always saved La Sylphe for last. First that brunette one would come out; she would have on a black nightgown, and gradually she would take it all off, except those T-shaped panties they wear and a pair of gilded horns on her breasts—no straps or anything. When the tourists are not standing right over me, I can see them all: Five Beautiful Girls. There's Allumette and Bonnie Belle (she doesn't work steady, though) and there's Slipper Ann, sometimes called Slippery, who has a thing about shoes and owns more than a hundred pair. Then comes the girl who does the Hawaiian pineapple strip, Aloha and Tortoise-Shell, called that, the guys in the Quarter say, because she has such a hard back.

Then came La Sylphe. When she came out on the stand the men would croak like frogs. I've seen them come back night after night for a week—dead-looking men with gouged-out eyes, pushing their fat stomachs up close to the bar, and glueing their eyes to her like they were stone drunk, only they weren't. Sometimes they would bring their wives with them, scrawny women from their own hometown who didn't know the score, who never understood that the men were not thinking of them afterwards in bed at all—but of La Sylphe.

I thought of La Sylphe too. I thought of her every night. I would fall asleep thinking of her breast under my hand. Or of her belly; it had a white streak all around it, like lightning had struck her once, and the curve of her back was like horseflesh. I would just lie in bed and sweat, thinking about it. Then one night I dreamed she came to my room and said, "You're not a bad guy for a cripple." That was when I decided to use my money to see if I could get La Sylphe. For years I'd been saving it, nickel by nickel, quarter by quarter. Then dollar by dollar. That is why I never moved from my room on Dauphine Street. It was the cheapest room in the Quarter and every now and then the Vieux Carré Commission of New Orleans would talk about tearing the building down and "restoring" it, patio and all, but they never did, so I stayed.

In the first place, I had a gas burner there on Dauphine Street, and the bed was low enough for me to get in by myself. All I needed to do was grab hold of the metal bar and haul myself in. It was an old metal bed, and somebody had sawed off the top part of the legs to make it more modern. That is where I kept my money.

I bought some elbow plumbing pipe, to slip into the hollow legs of the bed, like one empty can will fit into another. Pieces just one inch in diameter fit perfectly. I told the guy I was going to make a new kind of rat trap, and he just laughed. "Sure need 'em around here," he said. The pieces fit very tight inside the legs of the bed, and it would have taken a strong arm like mine to wrench them out.

Nobody would of dreamed that a beggar like me would have had all that money. But I was careful. I never drank or smoked, and winters I slept in my clothes to save on heat. And always I thought, if you save enough you can get off the Street.

Al would come by in the morning to put me in my chair. Al is a World War Two vet. He was cut up a lot and he's not much good for anything, but he would come help me into my chair mornings. And sometimes we would have French coffee the way he liked it, strong. I made it myself. I did all my own cooking. That saved a lot. I ate canned soups a lot; you can add things to them, like beans soaked overnight, or hominy grits. And there's plenty of cheap fish in New Orleans—catfish, herring, squid. I got so I could bone a herring so it would fit right in the skillet, flat as a pancake. So I got along all right before La Sylphe came up to me that time. And I didn't just live on fish either. I had a metal box-stove, the kind you slip right over the burner, and one time Al and I baked a lobster he swiped at the market. We laughed a lot that time and weren't lonely. Because that is the main thing, feeling lonely.

That is why when La Sylphe crossed over to my side that morning about dawn, it was like the sun fell into my lap. I looked up at her and for a minute I was so scared I couldn't say anything. My first thought was that she knew all about how I'd been watching her and thinking about her and that she didn't like it—that she was going to tell me to change my spot on the Street, I was getting on her nerves, something like that.

But she just stood up straight and tall, like a runner taking deep breaths. She had on those tight pants they wear when they're off-stage, and high-heeled wedgies without straps to them, and a red sweater that was no sweater at all. She said: "Did you see a big, heavy guy out here— he had a camera with him, took moving pictures?" She checked her watch, then, a big watch with leather straps like a man's. The man she was looking for was obviously a tourist. No guy from the Quarter would lug around a camera, especially in a night club. But anyway I hadn't seen any such person, and I was always aware of the finks who hung around waiting for her after work. More often it was just her guy Batchelli who picked her up. So my guess was, the guy hadn't waited for her at all, but after taking some pictures of her had lost himself in the crowd. I could see she was disappointed and I thought right away, maybe this is my chance. She might never get up that close again.

I lowered my voice so nobody else in the Street would know that she was getting fixed up with a street beggar. I was afraid if she thought anybody'd heard us she'd have to say no out of pride.

When I made my bid I saw her gold-colored eyes flare up like the painted blue edge around them had caught fire. I could see she could hardly believe a guy like me would have so much. It made me feel real good, like I was doing something big.

"Where do you live?" she asked with a funny look, scared and hurried, as if taking that much money was some kind of crime and she was afraid she'd be caught.

I gave her my number and the time was set for four o'clock, a good two hours before we went to work on the Street. I wanted plenty of time, because I knew she would need to get used to me. The last time a woman saw me undressed was at the county hospital, when I had pneumonia. The nurses kept changing every day, like they couldn't stand the sight of me. Then there came one who'd been working in the terminal wards. The first day she made a point of undressing me entirely and she stood there staring at me a while. Then she rubbed the S-shaped bone in my chest with her little finger and said, as if nobody was there to hear her: "It's just like somebody took him and twisted him right around . . ."

Once La Sylphe had agreed to come, I tried to keep her standing there a minute talking to me, so that maybe Hawaii Jim would see us just talking together, like friends. But she was already looking up the Street, clutching her big handbag in both hands, like she was afraid someone would grab it. I noticed then that her hair was not really gold-colored like her eyes but that there were dark roots, like shoots pushing from the earth. A small line of impatience, or maybe it was anger at that guy with the camera, had formed above her mouth, one of those deep lines that later gets to be like creased leather in greedy old men. But she was beautiful to me . . . especially her hands, which were long and straight and the pointed nails were painted white, like moonstones.

"I guess the dirty liar's gone," she said at last.

Her still thinking about that tourist made me sick-jealous, but I just laughed as if I really did think I was God's-gift-to-women, and said: "That's all right, honey, you got me." I thought she might laugh or put her hand on my head or come back with a real snappy line, like a trooper. But instead, she looked down at me like she could spit, then she started clicking away on her high heels as fast as she could go. I watched her legs from where I sat, strong curved instruments, made of ivory.

"See you later!" I called after her, casual-like, but it was meant to close our deal.

By the way she looked at me I knew I would have to show that money the moment she got there. So I went home and pried loose the pipe from inside the bedpost, which I hadn't done in years. I even took out some rolls that hadn't been touched since I first started on the Street. I noticed then that the bed was beginning to rust a little and some of the bills had a powdery feel. The weevils had eaten through the newspaper I had stuffed in at the top, and had even penetrated some of the older money, some that I got when I first went on the Street.

I took it all out, all the bills, and cleaned them carefully with alcohol. I rolled the fifties tight toward the heart of the roll—I keep them tight as spools of tape, the twenties and tens on the outside. That way, even, if there was a fire that melted the bed, the big ones would be saved. You know a book will burn on the outside, then snuff out toward the middle. In the other leg of the bed I always kept my cash till I could change it to bills at the bank. I went only once a month, to a different teller each time, so they never caught on how much money I had. Maybe I could have left the Street years ago but I wanted to be sure that when I left I'd never have to come back.

But now I needed a lot. After all, I figured La Sylphe had expensive tastes. She was used to being taken to the La Louisiane and Antoine's and Galatoire's and all those places I'd never been. She'd probably want a drink first, I thought, the best Scotch or maybe brandy. Maybe I'd better have both. . . . And then I'd have dinner brought in, like they do in hotels. But the main thing was to have the place clean, so I asked Al to help me. He pretended not to notice anything as we put on new sheets as white as milk and I made him empty all the trash around, even in the halls. Then Al gave me a good wash, all the time pretending not to see what was going on. I didn't want him to be there when she came in, though, so when it got to be nearly four I hurried him out.

I was so nervous I kept breaking out in a sweat till I worried about the wash Al had given me not doing me any good; so I tried to calm down by counting the squares in the linoleum; but one shape just blurred into another and I couldn't make out what I was counting. I noticed at the last minute that my nails were not clean and I was in a panic to get them clean by myself. But I finally did.

About this time there was a little tap-tap on the door. It was Amy, of course. She always taps that way, like it's a game we're playing that maybe I got up and walked away. She said there was a real old-fashioned organ-grinder with a monkey parked in front of the French Coffee House: would I like to see it? She said maybe an organ-grinder really enjoyed playing his music, the monkey was so cute, he must be company for the Italian guy with the handle-bar mustaches. She asked me did I think he was really Italian? I could see what she was driving at, but I just said angrily that when I left the Street I was going to leave it for good, I wasn't going to go tinkle-tinkle around the country with a trick monkey and a fake handle-bar mustache. I said I was tired of fakes, even myself. I said I was a fake too.

She took my good hand and looked at it. "You have such a strong hand, Billy," she said. "I bet you could hold me up flat and lift me to the ceiling."

There was something about her calling me Billy at that moment that made me almost sick. It was as if I'd forgot my name was Billy and thought it really was Duncan Phyfe. And besides I was mad at her for taking such a damnfool time to come in, so I said, "Yeah, a strong hand like that could be very useful. I could get a job holding the torch for the Statue of Liberty."

She looked me full in the face then, very strange, and then those straight-out eyelashes, like a doll's, shut down over her face like the Quarter itself, sliding down all its beautiful pastel shutters, closing to tourists. Then she picked up my hand and cradled it a minute like a baby. "Billy-Billy," she said.

Then I could hear La Sylphe's wedgies clicking out in the yard. "Run along now, kid," I said, my throat like clay. "I got things to do." So she went. I don't know whether she saw La Sylphe coming up the old patio or, if she did see, whether she had any idea where La Sylphe was going. Anyway the sight of La Sylphe put Amy completely out of my mind.

She wasn't dressed up or anything. In fact, she was wearing a kerchief over her hair and slacks and carrying a small purse in her hand, like she was trying to let on she'd just slipped out to the grocery. Before she could say anything I handed her the money, and I saw the deep line above her mouth soften into a shadow as she counted it. She was tense all right, but not at all scared, like I would of thought. She didn't look so much like a kid from the Nebraska cornfields, but as if she'd been around a long time. When she unzippered, though, she was beautiful. Her zippers worked silently, as if they'd been oiled. The only sound she made was of somebody holding their breath.

I was trembling all over, and I thanked my stars for that strong right arm so she didn't have to help me on to the bed or anything.

She didn't do much talking at first, but afterwards she told me about what happened in Nebraska and how she wanted to get off the Street. If she could just make it fast enough, she said, she would open a little restaurant in Las Vegas and be set for life.

At first I was just looking at her, I hardly heard a word she said. It was that good to see a thing so perfect. Her skin was almost bronze, with two wider circles of light above where her clothes evidently filtered the sun. The notion crossed my mind as I squatted there, keeping myself covered, that she was just like those cornfields she came from, full of silk hair and golden light. Only her using herself like that was like shucking the leaves back to find the corn was ruined.

Maybe it was thinking crazy thoughts like that that triggered it off, but all of a sudden we started hating each other. I have thought it out over and over, but still I cannot remember what started it. Maybe it was not really thinking about cornfields at all; maybe it was Amy and her ill-timed visit. Because while Amy had been telling me about my strong hand and how I could lift her to the ceiling, I'd had a sort of pain in my chest, exactly at the curve of the bone—how shall I say it?—a "sorrow." I guess that's what love is, and all the stories about happy love are a fake. It was too bad that the thing, whatever it was, had to grow in me just that time La Sylphe was there.

And so there was La Sylphe lying there with one arm behind her head, I could see she enjoyed letting me look at her, and her greedy fingers playing with the money I'd made in my own little hell. I felt she was flaunting herself, that she wanted me to feel my ugliness. And I started thinking what a stupid animal she was living that way when she had a body that was as near perfect as a body can be. I guess I started thinking of what a person can do if he's born with two arms and two legs just like everybody else. So I hated her as if she were some sort of scab on the face of the earth, deforming it. It was as if her kind of ugliness only made mine worse.

So I must have been the one who said the first word, maybe wanting to get even with her for using herself like garbage. Then she lashed into me. She said I stank, that all cripples stank, that they never washed, and if there was anything in this world that made her sick to look at it was a cripple. She spat on the floor and said if I ever told anyone she'd been there, she'd have her man, Batchelli, tear me to pieces.

I just sat in the middle of the bed till she was through. Then I jeered at her for saying cripples stank. I said she was capable of any filth for money and she knew it. She screamed at me that there wasn't enough money in the world to make her look at me again.

She had the door open, and at that moment it was worth all I had to get her back, to humiliate her. I named a fantastic figure, so much money that I felt myself grow cold I was so scared at what I'd said, even though I still had more, and at the same time the "sorrow" seemed to burst in my chest, it hurt so bad. But I had the satisfaction of seeing her stop short, her back up against the wall, like her legs had turned weak.

"You don't have it. . . ." she said, drawing in her breath.

I knew that to remove the pipe in front of her would be a dead give-away. But at that moment I hated her more than I loved money. It was like a revelation, almost like a conversion, that you could feel that deep about anything. Just then money was my only weapon against her, but it made me stronger than she was. Because when she saw that coil of money rolled tight as tape she dropped her purse down on the chair. And it was as I'd said: she was capable of anything for money. Only this time there was absolute silence, like we were digging a grave. And I'll never forget the look on her face when she saw the money. It was the look of a murderer, a madman, who sees you have food in your hand and he's starving. His first impulse is to kill you and tear the stuff out of your hands, but he has to pretend to be sane long enough to get near you. . . . I ought to have known by that look that I should have cleared out of Dauphine Street that night. Because the next night she and a couple of her boys broke open my lock, took every dollar and set fire to the bed.

I have not seen La Sylphe in the Quarter since then, so maybe she made it to Las Vegas after all. But several people have told me they've seen her around, that Batchelli beat her and left her for dead, taking all the money.

But it was strange what happened afterwards. I never said a word to anybody about it, so I don't know how it got around. Maybe La Sylphe herself told it. Anyway, it got around the Quarter, and guys who'd never talked to me before began asking me for a match and the first thing I knew they'd be talking to me about La Sylphe. It was like they were just waiting for a chance to talk.

I have moved to a better place, with heat all winter. I still have my spot on the Street, and I do pretty good, but somehow I don't save much. I don't cook anymore, it's too lonely eating in my room. So I go to Holmes' now and then; a bunch of us guys have got the habit of eating there. And I am buying a La Scala accordion, the best; you can play it pretty good with one hand.

Beating and Beatitude

FOR DAVID A.

Story this the title of . . . Beatitude and Beating. Written ever have I story the first.

Very well stories write can't I. No. Very well stories *tell* can't I, mean I. Tongue mine over stumble I. Lost get I and up balled all become words mouthful by.

Well fairly stories *write* can I (below see please), and audience mine hold I think.

You for a clue provided this all, way secret head mine enter for you to and story mine and me understand better. Know you, understood to be want I. Believed and.

Beautiful was it did I. Good it felt and how.

Beating and Beatitude . . . the title of this story. The first story I have ever written.

I can't write stories well. No. I mean I can't *tell* stories very well. I stumble over my tongue. Words by the mouthful become all balled up and I get lost.

I can *write* stories fairly well, however, and I think I hold my audience.

I write stories fairly well because I do a lot of rewriting. I have to. I suffer from a condition known as dyslexia. That means reading—and sometimes even writing—backwards. Occasionally I *see* things backwards as well . . . actions: things people have done or even what I have done or am doing myself. The words "begin at the beginning" have no meaning for me. I begin at the end. It's easier that way. Thus my life is backward. I wasn't born first. I died. I move slowly over the years toward birth. You other poor stiffs have nothing to look forward to but death.

All this is by way of providing a clue for you, a secret way for you to enter my head and better understand me and my story. I want to be understood, you know. And believed.

I tell only true stories.

This is a true story. It is *not* fiction. Thus I may be accused of something one day, sued, put in jail for what I am about to tell you.

You, too, for you are my accomplice. We work together.

I am one of twins and my brother and I mirror one another almost perfectly. The only difference is when we speak. I stammer and sometimes it is hard for me to control my saliva. That is the way you tell us apart: you ask us to speak to you. The one who stammers is me; the other, the "bright penny," as my mother calls him, is my brother. He's a genius: he speaks, he reads, he writes perfect words in perfect sentences. I . . . have a connection missing somewhere. My brain is good but my tongue and eyes reverse and jumble the messages. It is a handicap I have learned to live with over the years. And my brother as well . . . He has learned to live with it, even though he won't admit it.

Like most twins, we have always been very close, and we were especially so during the early years when we were hardly more than a couple of toddlers together, playing the games we played and growing up in the light and warmth of our mother's love. She treated us as equals—as, indeed, we were then—and there was no hint of any rivalry between us. My brother was a little quicker than I, but I was able to hold my own and get my way now and then simply by throwing a fit. This became the prime distinguishing feature between us at first: I was the temperamental one. I was also the one who woke late at night and threw the entire household into chaos.

In those days it was never a question of "I" or "you" between my brother and myself, but of "we," and what one did the other was sure to imitate. We ate together, slept together, went visiting together, and even took our baths together on Saturday night. We played the tricks and games twins play together, substituting our bodies for one another and fooling our friends. The game always ended when I became carried away with myself, actually believed that I was my brother, and tried to speak.

"Oh, Dull Penny it's you!"

"Oh, Dull Penny why do you speak?"

"Oh, Dull Penny why are you so dull?"

I hated them all but especially I hated my name. "What's in a name?" you may ask. And Dull Penny answers, "Thing every a name in is. Thing every."

I loved my brother very much but hated him for what he had that I did not: words. We used to stand and stare at one another as into facing mirrors, he wiping his chin of saliva that was not there, and I, dull penny, worshiping him. When he moved his lips I moved mine, but what came out was not the same.

Sometimes, when I am feeling very sad and depressed, I think he stole my brain when we were younger, or else God made a mistake and gave my mother two babies but only one with a head on it. Why should everything be so much easier for him than it is for me? And why is talking about him like speaking a foreign language, the words and phrases of which are so complicated they send my head spinning? That is why I stammer at times, and why more often than not I come up with the simplest sentences to describe my most complex feelings about him. I don't have all the words, and many of the verbs and adjectives are still unlearned. A mystery. What people call prepositions and conjunctions are especially difficult and often I simply give up and slip into my dyslexia again. Then, reading or writing or speaking is like being caught in the blades of a machine. Each word is a knife and I cut myself just thinking about how they go together, what they mean, or where you are or are not supposed to use them. Bright Penny laughs and says that I should take elocution lessons.

I had a dream once, and I've had the same dream on and off for most of my life. Bright Penny and I are walking along a beach when we come upon a baby gorilla lying on the sand. It has neither arms nor legs and its tongue has been ripped out. It is dying apparently. I used to think that Bright Penny was the gorilla and I the head-less baby mentioned earlier, because I could always do things with my limbs—throw a rock, kick a ball—better than he could. Now I am not so sure. Maybe I am both dreams.

I love my brother and I love the baby gorilla lying on the sand. And it has always been my hope that I would never have to choose between them.

As mentioned, what began in the beginning for us as absolute equality soon became inequality when certain members of the family noticed that my brother was the bright one of the two and I the dullard. For a time then, I got more than my share of attention because it was thought I needed more. As the gap between us widened, however, and my brother's talents came more and more to the fore, the flow reversed itself and my mother began to put more of her love where she thought it would do the most good. My brother, her "bright penny" and great hope for the future, once again began to reap his fair share of her affections.

When the time came for him to go to school, he went to school, while I stayed home getting duller and duller with the passing years. I saw him off each morning and waited patiently for his return at night, passing the time in one of the two hideaways we had on the hill behind our house. I lay in the bushes like a thief ready to steal the riches of his mind. When I saw him coming, laden with books and his eyes bright with some new piece of information he had learned that day, I ran to meet him brandishing my weapons and shouting voiceless threats. "Your intelligence or your life," I wanted to say, but the words always came out wrong.

"Hello, Dull Penny," he would answer. "What did you do today?"

"N N N Nothing did I," I would stammer. "Nothing. You for waited I."

He would smile indulgently, hand me his books, and we would start up the hill toward the house together, I a step or two behind in the position of slave and beast of burden to a twin brother. I didn't mind because I loved to be of use to him and to be used. Employed. It gave me a sense of worth I would not have had otherwise, and I especially delighted in helping him with his studies whenever he would let me. I brought him fresh sheets of paper from the hall closet to write on, for example, new ink for his pen, or a fist-full of No. 2, Mongol Pencils, newly sharpened and ready to use. I was perfectly content to sit for hours at a time watching him read his books, copy out his lessons, and do his complicated math problems. I listened and listened to him speak his beautiful words to my mother.

To a regular school I never did go but many books backwards I have read.

My brother's books.

And I wore his old clothes when he was finished with them. I had to. We were poor and my mother a woman alone in the world trying to live and make do on what a woman earns. Bright Penny got the new clothes because Bright Penny went out into the world and was seen. He went to school. I stayed home lurking about the house all day like an idiot. As we grew older, his freedoms and privileges increased while mine remained constant or shrunk. He played all the sports at school I was better at and studied subjects I did not even know existed. He brought home grades and won honors, took out girls and even had an allowance for awhile. He had a part-time job and earned money. When we went to church he prayed while I could but mumble, and he even sang in the choir. Sang! I knew that I would never, ever be able to sing. It was all I could do just to speak a few words without stumbling over myself, and my voice was so warped and rusty from disuse that it was painful to listen to. I sang with his voice instead, or so I imagined, spoke with his lips, and thought with his brain. I made love to the girls he loved with his body. And I begrudged him every pleasure he experienced directly I could only experience second-hand. Most of all I hated him for the full life he led and I longed to have one of my own.

When he finally finished high school I thought, "Well, now things will right themselves again and we will be as we were before: equal and identical in every way and sharing the same life. There will be no more imbalance, either in what he gets or what I receive, and we will take from the family only that which we need. Our shares of love and money will be equal and we will have the happy life back again."

This is what I thought but I was a fool.

"Bright Penny is very smart and Bright Penny will be a doctor," my mother said one day. "Bright Penny will go away to the university. Dull Penny will stay home and help with the chores."

"More school?!" I thought. "Why does he need more school? How much can a person learn? To school want I . . . I want to school . . . Learning . . ."

He went away to school and I stayed home to help with the chores. Everything was as it had been, except that when he left it was as if he were gone for good this time, and he did not return each night to do his lessons as in the past. He was in another city, living with another family, and when we heard from him it was by mail: long, rambling letters I could not read very well containing a lot of big words I did not understand. I missed him terribly.

As the weeks turned into months and the months a year, we skimped and saved and made do with very little so that my brother might have all the money he needed to do whatever it was he was doing. We even expanded the garden and began to sell a bit of the surplus around the neighborhood, and we cut a lot of corners so that he could get his education and be a success in the world. "He was the bright one in the family," my mother kept saying. "And he must be given his chance." I said nothing. As the seasons passed, I did nothing. Only the chores. I became expert at emptying the garbage and beating rugs. I hoed corn and hawked radishes from door to door. I pulled weeds and then burned them, once almost setting the house on fire, and I went down to the mailbox each day to get the mail. I had long conversations with no one and did not pass the time very productively. I waited . . . for my brother probably, but maybe for someone else. I withdrew. When a man came to the house one day to speak with my mother, I stared at him stupidly.

"Your roof needs repairin', ma'am," he said.

"Yes, you're right," she answered, and the two discussed what should be done about our roof. He was a carpenter apparently, but had no helper and worked on a day-to-day basis traveling about town. He was old but not too old and had a droopy moustache that seemed to grow right into his nose. He was friendly.

"Will the boy help?" he asked when they came to the part about money.

"Yes," she answered. "But you mustn't expect too much of him."

"I won't," he said, and I spent the better part of that afternoon fetching nails for him, helping him cut and haul shingles, and generally lending a hand. He was very patient with me, and when he wanted something he called me Penny. *Not* Dull Penny. But Penny. It made all the difference.

At the end of the day he offered me a job saying, "I know you're not as bright as your brother, Penny, but I think you ought to do something in this life and a job as carpenter's helper might be pretty good for you. What do you say?"

"For to work as a carpenter I want," I stammered. "Helper's work and learning . . ."

He smiled broadly. "Well, good. Good. I know you speak in tongues, but I guess we'll get along okay." And he turned to my mother to make the necessary arrangements.

You should have seen the look on her face. It was beautiful, and right away I knew that I had something from her that I had not had in a long time: a different kind of love for one, but also hope and faith, belief, and a new, more positive interest in me as a human being and what I might or might not become in life. With this kind of support I knew that I could not possibly fail.

My first day on the job I did nothing but haul timbers and cut shingles at fifty cents an hour. I also kept my boss supplied with a good bucket-full of nails and did a lot of cleaning-up at the end of the day when we were finished working. He said that he would pay me more as soon as he could afford it and that my jobs would get more interesting as we went along.

After I had been with him for a week, he let me hold boards for him while he nailed, and at the end of two weeks I was practically nailing them myself. At the end of a month he called me over one day and began to teach me how to mark them off and cut them. "Penny, this is a fish-tape," he said, picking up a funny-looking, disc-like, object nearby, "and we use it to measure boards. This thing over here is a rule."

"Fish-tape, rule," I repeated, my eyes going from one to the other.

"That's right," he said. "Now you see these little lines they've got running up and down them? They're inches. There're twelve inches in a foot and three feet in a yard. If I tell you that I want a board six feet long, well all you do is take the fish-tape or the rule and mark it off: one, two, three, four, five, six. Do you understand?"

"Yes, sir. I count."

"That's right. And if I tell you I want six and a half feet you count to six and a half. You make a mark with this straight-edge here. It's called a square. When I put the board in a wall I use the square again to make sure it's straight and sometimes I use a spirit-level. You have to make sure all the boards are straight or else the house will turn out crooked. Do you understand?"

"Yes sir."

"Good."

Fish-tape, rule. Spirit-level. Feet and inches. For the first time in my life I was learning! I had a job. Money. I was growing a new set of arms and legs, and maybe even finding my tongue. I couldn't have been happier.

As I flourished my brother seemed to flounder, however, and our situations became much the reverse of what they had been. Although we had identical bodies, there was only one Life Force to be divided between us apparently, and when one brother had it the other did not. As hard as it is for me to say this, my brother became dull, or if not dull, at least confused, because he suddenly could not make up his mind about anything and spent his first two years at the university jumping from one course of study to another without being able to settle on any one subject. My mother said that it was a sign of the times and she was bitterly disappointed. I was shocked. He was her "bright hope for the future" and my idol. We didn't know what to do about him.

And then he decided to come home.

To get money, he said, and to travel.

To get *our* money, mine and my mother's. And maybe he came home for something else as well.

Now let me tell you something. A strange thing happened while he was away. Not only did I find my purpose in life, but I became much stronger than he physically as well. Some kind of compensation had taken place. He still had the brain between us maybe, but I most definitely had the body. In the couple of years he was gone I must have gained ten or fifteen pounds on him. I was a tiger and you should've seen the arms on me. They were the arms of a young gorilla.

I also had a very different mental attitude. I still spoke in riddles, of course, but there was something going on behind those riddles now and I was sure he would notice. "Look," I planned to say to him, "I'm a new man. Treat me like one. I have a job, you don't. I can do things. Let's help one another. I'll teach you about my job if you'll teach me about words."

"You build words just like you build a house," he will say. "Look: this is a sentence. This word here is a subject, and the other one is a verb. Every subject has a verb and vice versa. The verb tells you what the subject is doing."

"You build a house like a sentence," I'll answer. "Look: this is the foundation . . ."

I also planned to tell him about the mysteries of the spirit-level and about how, if you hit a nail just right, the head follows an invisible line and the nail goes in without bending.

The day he came home I was waiting for him in the old hiding-place on the hill above the house right where I waited for him in the old days. When I saw him coming I wanted to rush down and greet him, carry his books again, help him with his studies, and bring him pen and ink so that he could write all the beautiful things he wrote in his notebooks. I wanted to talk to him as we'd never talked before. I wanted to *communicate* with him. I hung back and waited instead. I was very nervous and the words were already beginning to ball up inside, the blades of the machine beginning to cut.

He came up the road to the house, circled it once, hesitated a second, and then walked right in without knocking. He went to his room and began unpacking one bag and packing another. He had many books and papers but very few clothes. He looked tired. Old. And his face had the lean, ascetic look of a scholar. His hair was down to his shoulders.

I wanted to bow down my head and worship him.

I wanted to kill him.

"My life," a voice cried within. "Life mine."

I went down the hill to meet him. My brother. Yes. Brother mine to meet two years after and lifetimes. Stood we face to face staring as if strangers at: twin looking twin into but seeing not what twin before seen had.

"Penny Dull, hello," said he. "What doing you have been since last saw you I?"

"W W W Working," said I. Laughed he but cry wanted to I.

"Working? Well money earning then must you be. Money any have you, Penny Dull?"

My head shook I.

"Come, come," said he. "Take me for what, do you? Penny dumb, Penny Dull don't be. To go away again money need I."

To speak tried I but come not words would. Head mine huge felt, and gorilla baby thought I saw I again.

"Hear me did you, Penny Dull?"

Hit him once did I, twice maybe, but hurt him really don't think I. To bruise only and cut one little cut on cheek. Lay something broken at our feet, shattered and. Doppelganger mine, I think, or freak. Turned I then and away walked quickly.

Beautiful was it did I, and truth. Good it felt. But brother mine impossible it is I think again to meet. And God, oh God, how to speak?

Silences

Christmas Eve, and the advice columns
are filled with letters from people wanting to hear
if it's true, a farmer told their great aunt
that tonight the animals are restless,
noisy, as if they know. Some claim they speak.
I spent one holiday
with a friend who could barely get through
six words without some consonant sticking
in his throat. While people looked on, silent,
he'd choke out the fragments of a word.

With one foot twitching out-of-time to the words
like a bad drummer trying to catch up,
each sentence could take such effort.
It was too delicate to ask about
despite his manner and the jokes at work.
He could sing perfectly though, things like
Silver Bells and *It's Beginning to Look
a Lot Like Christmas*, the same few lines
in a voice smooth as on a tv special.
I was amazed and figured it for a joke.

His children must have agreed not to let on.
He worried, he said, when the eldest
nearly three, still hadn't said one word.
Until he caught them both, secretly
talking whole sentences. In front of people
his wife tried finishing his sentences,
as if he'd lost the conversation's drift.
I cultivated looking deep in thought.
The children seemed to ignore him. Over dinner
they avoided speaking with any grownup,
chattering uneasily to each other,
a game they'd tired of.
I found them distant, irritating.

Sometimes it was only a hesitation
the way, middle-aged, you might regret
never playing good basketball, pause,
then go on. Each of us pretended
not to notice, or that he might not know,
to save him embarrassment.
It was an awkward silence between friends.
Yet he could rise with anger,
a sudden fluency terrifying as a miracle,
arguing full-volume with a cop
who stopped us on the sidewalk
while I prayed his stammer would return.

The Glen

Over the sound of her dishes clacking lightly in the soapy water, she could hear the sound of Harmon's voice. It was his third voice—neither the usual quick tense run of speech, nor even the slower, more accentuated tones in which he spoke to Cora, but his slowest, quietest yet most emphatic speech—as if he put each word, with a soft pause, up for special inspection. Soap bubbles winked and died on the plate which Jessie held still for a minute, listening to that voice wheedle Cora to accept the words. "'You!' said the Caterpillar contemptuously, 'Who are *you!*'"

Futilely and masochistically, as she might have pressed a great dark bruise, she raised her eyes to the little mirror flat on the wall over the kitchen sink, and there she saw them. Cora sat in her small mahogany chair with the cane seat and back. Her red curls shone faintly, under the edge of the firelight's motion; her mouth, slack and open, sagged a little more than usual, in distrait attention; her hands, with their short square fingers whose nails Jessie had cut that morning, lay curled upward, flaccid in her lap. The tomato juice had gone through her bib and there was a great oblong stain over her chest.

"'I don't remember things as I used—and I don't keep the same size for ten minutes together!'"

Suddenly Jessie noticed that Harmon was wearing a sweater, and this instantly brought the autumn to her as had neither the cold steady rain nor the shiver of the dripping asters outside the window. She glanced at the seasonless clock for comfort. Winter seemed at her throat in a leap, and after she had dried the last dish she raised her eyes again to the little mirror—this time to exchange with herself a long, reserved look. The brown eyes, bright and clear as the mercury in which they were reflected, regarded her. She was four years older than Harmon, but she doubted if this knowledge would have affected him had it been his; which it was not. Her fingers reached for the light switch, but lingered a moment, as though she and her reflection had a last important image to communicate.

"'One side will make you grow taller, and the other will make you grow shorter.'"

It was almost cruel, though of course Harmon's dark, obsessive drive would never see that. The child was not listening, she was unable to listen; but tranced by the familiar voice linking its sounds for her, she gazed with her dull sea-blue eyes into the prancing fire. Jessie could see the skin of her fat little face, that skin which together with her hair was the only

Reprinted by permission from *A Walk with Raschid and Other Stories* (Jackpine Press); copyright © 1978.

gift in all her grossness. Her stepmother was close enough to see its texture. Translucent, fresh as petals, it flushed and paled in delicate shelltints. In one of her passions, it flamed like a fury. Harmon's voice was reaching some sort of climax:

"'Alice remained looking thoughtfully at the mushroom for a minute, trying to make out which were the two sides of it.'"

Harmon bent over to show Cora the picture, but her face did not change. He said slowly, "She's going to *eat* it and *change*!" With surprise, Jessie saw a shade of expression cross Cora's face; her eyelids squinted.

"'And now which is which?' she said to herself, and nibbled a little of the right hand bit . . .'"

Cora had begun to breathe quickly; a thin thread of saliva looped to the collar of her yellow dress over the bib. Her eyes turned from the fire to fasten on her father's lips. Harmon glanced at her and, delighted, repeated, ". . . and nibbled a little of the right hand bit to try the effect."

Cora began to rock lightly in her chair and a sound came from deep in her throat. In the kitchen Jessie switched out the light. Anything to do with eating, she thought with an angry hopelessness. She took off her apron came round and into the room, and slipped into the big wicker chair by the lamp.

"She was shrinking rapidly: so she set to work at once to eat some of the other bit . . ."

So there they were, arranged in their places: the fire, the rain, the child, and Harmon's pausing voice.

Long after Cora was in bed, about ten, the rain stopped; suddenly they could hear the rush of the little stream to one side and below them.

Until a few nights ago, since the quarrel, the late evenings had held an awkward quality; it was as though they brought echoes. But the change which had come in Philadelphia and altered Jessie's world again—already too altered in the past year—had freed them both, though Harmon knew nothing of it. For Jessie herself it was undefined. As soon as this change had showed itself in her voice, in her renewed ability to laugh, it had been reflected in their eagerness to touch each other. It was as though it was Harmon who was reprieved.

"It's stopped raining," she said. She went to the door and opened it, and the cold damp rush of the night air chilled her face and her bare arms.

She could feel him behind her, and, yes, there came his hand on the back of her neck. At that minute the moon tore loose from its black cloudbank and rode out into bare sky. The smell of dead leaves, of wet earth, swirled round them and Jessie thought, exultant, "I'm not afraid of it now. I am stronger. I can wait for whatever I must wait for." And she spun round and pressed her face to Harmon's. He caught her to him so quickly that she gasped. He slammed the door with his left hand, and for the first time in weeks, locked together they moved softly into the room where the moon picked out patches on the counterpane.

The next morning the sun burned off the mists early, and by the time the Buick bounced down the drive ruts and, beyond the white rail fence, towards the city, it was warm. Jessie went to see what Cora was doing before she let herself take a final cup of coffee into the sun on the porch steps.

The little girl was on the floor in her room, squatting in a bar of sunshine, moving about the brown nutshells she had brought into the house yesterday. The smooth arc of her elbow and the red curls on her neck might have belonged to any child, who would now look up from this baby play and smile and greet her stepmother. But it was Cora, and she had no intention, even, of making one of her sounds—she seldom did, except in distress. She was absorbed in moving, very slightly, the shells: first so, and then almost back, and then back. It drove Jessie wild to watch her—the sheer stupid hopelessness of the play, which could not even be called play at all, but was some sort of lost and imbecile task; she could feel the nerves tingle with revulsion all down her spine.

She went out softly, turning the key in the lock behind her. The coffee could wait. Suddenly she must walk somewhere very fast, even if only for a few minutes. In the house, she could never let Cora run loose; she might squat there for hours, altering the position of her nutshells, or she might equally well pull the contents out of Jessie's drawer, or crush a brown raw eggshell in her fingers. Outside she was all right. She never went toward the road, seldom now even to the glen, which she had taken to so in the summer's heat. In August when she had not been lying in the cool dirt under the house, like a small white panting bitch (Jessie had even given up replacing the lattice), she was clumsily and carefully trying out the little glen, cutting her feet on its rocks, staining her shorts with crosses and weeds, falling flat on her face in the stream's inches of water, from which she came dripping in excitement, making her noises which were more convulsions of muscles than true sounds. Lately Jessie had been cautious in meeting the child's blue, clouded gaze. Once Cora had dropped asleep in her small cane chair, and Jessie, looking at her for some moments, had noticed that the lids were after all parted. Inexplicably, as she watched, Cora began plunging and almost grunting in fright, flinging from her chair and catapulting herself out of the room and all the way into Harmon's closet, where, a minute later, she had faced her stepmother as though Jessie were a stranger, and a bad stranger at that. Jessie was horrified. She spent a quarter of an hour in overtures, and finally Cora, as though Jessie had been one of those night-shapes which terrify, only to resolve themselves into a familiar lampshade or table-cover, had ended on the floor with her head in Jessie's lap. Cora seemed to forget this; Jessie did not. Sensing a true danger, she redoubled her efforts to please. In the first place, her passion for smoothness, for being wonderful, came first; but under it, deeper and wider, was the knowledge that, whichever way the cat jumped, Cora's friendliness or trust was absolutely essential.

Cora had taken to Jessie immediately; her vitality, the sort of animal friendliness produced by health and self-assurance, had drawn the child. Perhaps that was why and when Cora began to get on badly with Sue; perhaps her mind could hold only two affirmative figures. Or perhaps, as she became, irremediably, no baby, but a great girl almost seven, her rages, her balks, her vast stubborn tempers had killed Sue's knack with her. The coup de grace had been Jessie's trip to Philadelphia. When she had come back from those precious days, it had been to disaster. For all the hours of Harmon's daily absence, Cora had been in revolt: she fought and bit when Sue tried to dress her, wept soundlessly for hours, threw things; the last day before Jessie's return, Harmon had to stay home from work. A month earlier, Sue had quit the job, but five years had struck down roots and she had promised even to beg off from her next position to come now and then, or in an emergency. After Jessie's trip, her return was tacitly never mentioned again. Now Egbert, the next door farmer's son, came, not too unsuccessfully, every other afternoon, and sometimes for the evening.

Jessie went soundlessly through the kitchen, and down the steps onto the sparkling grass. The sumac bushes were a rich angry red, and the invisible stream sounded stronger after the rain. She knew this lovely pause before winter: it was the sort of day in which quail got up, mushrooms popped to the gold light, and squirrels turned nuts in their rapid, clawy paws. She walked, along the lawn to its east edge where the grass degenerated at the lip of the tiny ravine Harmon dignified by the name of glen. She stared down into its dampness with absentminded distaste. In summer it had been ferny, bosky, lush. Now it was moist and dark brown and full of things rotted by the early frosts; and winter, she knew, it would hold forever, with snow dirtying itself, and a cold mist of superficial melting as its response to the thin sun.

She had seen arbutus there in spring, she remembered, on the first day she had seen the house at all. And she remembered very clearly indeed how in August she had crouched on the rock, close to the tiny stream's line, which was then merely a bright movement over mud, on the morning of her first, her only, savage quarrel with Harmon. The realization that she had lost, that not then or ever would she be able to change Harmon, came back strong and bitter, even in her new confidence. At first she had thought it was because she had broached the thing badly, that Harmon had resented the mingling of love and pressure. She had still been glowing with the forbidden prospect of France, and she had approached her solution eagerly; but in the very midst of passion it had frozen Harmon. Harmon did not freeze like ice, but went soft with the rotten feel of stalks and stems still upright but touched by frost. But it was not until after the quarrel the next morning, until his pale set face in the oven of the Buick had disappeared down the drive, that she had faced things.

She had walked to just where she stood now. In that August haze of heat, cicadas were thick in the trees and three fields away the sound of a dog barking hung in the air. She had sunk down on just this rock. She remembered how her hand, cold with rage and fear, had felt it warm to the touch. The rage and fear had come with the quarrel, but it was only as she sat in the brutal heat, invisibly circling in her trap, that illumination after illumination came upon her in widening waves. At the center was her realization of Harmon's full wickedness, of how he had trapped her, of how both their lives were to be fed, as propitiation, to his insane sense of guilt. Odile's death and Cora's fate were somehow upon his head—it was as though that ghost of childbirth were standing at his shoulder, instructing him in his slavery. But widening her rage and despair came the small hard conviction that Harmon's primary reason for marrying her had been Cora; passion had been luck and secondary. And since passion was secondary, there was no way in which it could be utilized to circumvent his obsession.

It was difficult for her to realize this; she had great faith, if not in passion, in its techniques. While she had never seen herself as seeking Cora's head upon a charger, she had truly expected to control the disposition of the child—a kind and sensible disposition. Jessie came of people who were Wonderful; wonderful about circumstances and what circumstances brought to those they observed. If "Business as Usual" was not graved on their escutcheons, "Let us not be morbid" might have been. She admired wholly the women in her family: her aunt who had been wonderful when the fate of mosquito and primate alike had overtaken her young husband, in the form of an automobile crash; her mother, whose wonderfulness had never been better exemplified than when her husband, faced with a long and unpromising illness, had died from an overdose of his carefully regulated medicine. She knew that Harmon had not been wonderful about Odile, any more than he was wonderful about Cora. In this sense, he was wonderful about nothing, evidencing instead a neurotic strength of resistance to the healing powers of change, a stubborn fidelity to shades and shadows.

The shade of Odile lay on the bones of Cora's face—the wide forehead, the widely spaced eye-sockets, the short nose. There was in her face, Jessie rejoiced to note, no hint of Harmon. The shadow of Odile lurked in Harmon's study—in three bizarre cookbooks, in a book on herbaceous borders, on mushrooms, in a deframed photograph, bent at the corners, thrust into the back of the desk drawer.

That morning it had seemed to Jessie that life was to repeat itself, differently as usual; that she would have to divorce Harmon. It had seemed possible because of the rage, freshened at every turn by the thought of how easily he could *not* ruin everything in the wickedness of his monomania.

It had been coming, of course, to a head—but all within Jessie, who knew how to wait. She saw as her strongest card a benevolent game, her fortune in winning Cora—insofar as that flickering mind and obscure heart could be won. Time was what she had, and if she had hoped for a solution before winter set in, she could even face the house in the country, the most recent bastion in a steady retreat from life, through the snows and into the resolving spring, if need be.

It had been stupid, perhaps, for Harmon to tell her of the transfer offer; but actually, in the long run, what difference would it have made? He had told her so simply because it never occurred to him as a possibility.

"But *why?*" she asked. "Actually, why couldn't we?"

He had stared at her as though she were mad. It was late at night, in their bedroom, and with every window open the heat hung on them like a diffused weight.

"But it's in Lyons, in the city. If I couldn't manage Cora in town, can you imagine—in a foreign city—another language—a strange world . . . !"

She began to brush her hair again, and said gently, "But shouldn't we think about it? There are so many inquiries we could make. You speak French so well—perhaps Cora . . ."

He came up behind her and put his hand on her moving arm.

"Jessie, darling," he said. "Make it easy for me. Don't you realize how I'd have loved it—such a change . . . ?"

Her fingers discarded the brush and moved to the lamp. When it went out, they saw the moonlight on the floor. "I want what you want, Harmon," she said, almost inaudibly. "You know that."

"I do," he said, putting his hand on her small shoulders and drawing her back to lean against him. "By God, I do."

An hour later she had spoken again, and the false step had been made.

In the morning she had panicked, utterly panicked. On rising waves of comprehension, her fear, for the first and last time, had shaken her judgment. Harmon, knotting his tie, had turned, transfixed, at the shaking voice: "It's a disease—you're so warped now you can't *think* any more! What about Cora? What's her future? To hide out here with us, lying under the house, throwing her food about, ripping her clothes in her rages?"

He shot her a look, but she couldn't stop. "Don't you realize how life could be, for all of us? I've tried—you know that—you've *seen* it! Cora trusts me—I've never complained in all these five months. But she's *got* to be where they can help her—where they're prepared."

He came toward her slowly, and his voice was unnatural. "Jessie. You know Cora cannot be 'helped.' We've been through all that. Nothing is going to 'help' her, except maybe somehow, somewhere, love—love from people she belongs to. The kind of place you're talking about costs a fortune—far more than I have yet. And if it were free—do you hear me, Jessie?—if it didn't cost a goddamned cent, do you think—in your *presumption*," he suddenly, bitterly added, "that you can hand my child—Odile's child—over to strangers—snap the one link she's got with human beings—turn her into a cared-for animal? She's not an animal. She's not an idiot. She's a speechless, defective child. My child. And the child of her dead mother."

The perversity of it, the specious plausibility, stung her beyond endurance.

"You fool," she said slowly. "You married me to take care of Cora. You stupid, stupid fool."

He looked at her so long without speaking that she turned and walked dizzily out of the room. As she went past Cora's closed door, she could hear the bed beginning to rock. She heard Harmon slam the screen door, and, an instant later, his steps on the concrete floor of the garage. He'll have a headache, she thought, in a curious detachment, in this heat, with no breakfast. The sound of the car died away. Then, alone, Jessie was gripped by a single, lucid, intense fear: that she had gone too far.

Jessie poured cold milk into a clean solid jelly-glass, peeled a banana, put both on a small tray and went to Cora's room. The child's skin, fresh from sleep, was flushed with heat and her hair curled damply. She was pitching from side to side of the bed with a plunging motion, but she sat up as Jessie came in. Close to the bed, Jessie saw her eyes darken and the lids contract—it was her greatest sign of attention. Jessie set the jelly-glass of milk on the bedside table—it was almost certain to be spilled in the end, no matter what she did with it. Cora's hand reached out for the banana, the loose lips closed over its end. Jessie looked at the child, chewing. Those lips never kissed, or spoke; they only consumed.

"I have to go out, Cora," she said, gently and distinctly. "Jessie has to go out for a little while. I'll be back soon. I'll be back." She went to the door. "I'll turn the key," she said smiling. "So you'll be quite safe." Cora might have flung the banana, and the milk, too, on the floor—sometimes she would not be locked in. Then there would be a scene, or Jessie would stay in the house. But now the taste of the banana absorbed Cora. Jessie went out, turning the key quietly behind her. She went through the screen door, and although it was so early, the heat struck her heavily.

She walked over the browning grass into the shade at the lip of the glen. There was a flat-topped rock, poised solidly over that damp and still-green slope. Below, the small stream ran with a cool, busy sound. She sat there quietly, motionless. She rested, and gradually a peace and certitude welled up in her. She could feel power and purpose calming her pulse. She did not examine its sources. She rested in it gratefully. She sat and watched the ferns shiver lightly in a breath of air. A cardinal landed on the mud of the little streambed and ducked its head delicately into the thread of water. She thought of nothing, but scenes moved slowly across the heat: the out-of-state registry office where she and Harmon had been married at a chilly April ten o'clock; Cora's cereal oozing across the kitchen floor on the night she came into the house from her honeymoon; then she saw the gallant, steady, cool smile in her mother's eyes as they met hers outside the deathroom door. Never had Jessie asked a question.

Florida was too far, and Jessie found she wanted less to talk to her mother than to visualize her. She got Sue to come for four precious days, and she had left Harmon and gone back to Philadelphia. There was no idea, on the part of either her husband or herself, that this absence was the preliminary to a separation; but she knew, infallibly, that it would be a progressive strain for Harmon; as it might, in some degree, have been for her if she had doubted its outcome.

In Philadelphia, she had re-created, as far as possible, the life she and her mother had lived after her father's death and before her first marriage, staying in the same small good hotel, visiting exhibitions and vintage films, calling up a few old friends. She even renewed her faint acquaintance with French irregular verbs, feeling herself at times under the small steady smile of her mother's eyes. She would sit, in the sterile, grateful coolness of her air-conditioned room, the small green book in her lap. Harmon had destroyed his opportunity. But, Jessie said sensibly to herself, it was in these particular cards that there would be other chances. ". . . que j'acquiere . . . que j'acquisse . . . ," she said silently, while the room hummed on one tranquil note.

Soon she felt curiously renewed. When she came back, she knew exactly what she had to do—but she had not the faintest idea how she was to do it.

Now in the autumn morning, it struck her ferociously that she had only circled back, like a desperate animal, to this rock. Driven by the image of Harmon's sweater, she stared into the small audible stream, seeing in it the advancing winter, choked with snow, the rusted ferns broken by ice.

The sumac leaves were almost gone—the polished wood shone below the peaked, furry, crimson cones. Toadstools had sprouted overnight—three sprang from a rotted limb by her feet; one—tall, pale—lifted white gills straight from the ground. A squirrel sat up suddenly, near her, the bulbous eyes in his triangular head fixed, or not fixed, upon her, his paws shortened over his heart. As though a lever had been pressed in her head, what she gazed at was replaced by another scene: the firelight moving, Harmon's voice, Cora's gaze darkening and contracting. She sat still. The wet leaves shone around the sumac roots, in flowing bounds the squirrel leaped away. Though she sat absolutely motionless, inside her a great response had bloomed. It was as though an organic process had been initiated. She turned this response over and over in her mind, as the squirrel had turned its nut: at first she touched it gingerly, then as its strength and beauty became apparent, with growing confidence. From each angle it presented a flawless surface. Each flaw, each pitfall from which its predecessors had suffered, was finally and totally absent. It had a fatalistic perfection, as though she had been building it all her life, and as it turned before her eyes, fresh virtues, fresh inevitabilities were revealed.

She stood up abruptly, and for a moment the world pitched around her as though all her bearings were strange. She went over slowly and with her foot knocked off the three fat toadstools sprouting from the log, crushing them under her heel. She looked carefully and quietly at the rock, the rotting log, the tangle down toward the stream, the whole small lucid slope. Then she turned and went straight back to the house.

As though the one condition of her revelation was that she should not temporize, she went rather quickly through the door, through the living room, and into Harmon's study. She moved directly to the bookcase and took down an elaborate book with a slick, heavy jacket, illustrated in tones of ochre and acorn. She carried this to Harmon's desk, and sitting down, leafed through the pages, tentatively; but there was no difficulty. She had been absolutely right. The straight, regal shape rose on the page, pale and tall, single, springing from the earth, carrying its volva. She took Odile's book back to its shelf and began looking rapidly through all the three shelves, but fruitlessly. She looked around her, at the chair, the daybed: but there was no book lying about, and she went back into the living room, still looking rapidly around. Then she saw the red cover: it was on the little table by the fireplace.

She went to the wicker chair, sat down and opened the book, leafing lightly through until the picture arrested her. She looked at it for a moment; then she laid the book open on her lap, and sat there. She could hear the dog barking again, very faintly, and beyond the distant hedge and fence, the tires of a car passing.

Without warning, Cora began to pound on the bedroom door, heavily, as though she were hitting it with a wooden block—the noise was brutal. Jessie got up lightly, eagerly. "I'm coming, Cora!" she called, and she crossed to the door, turned the key and the handle, and stepped back. Cora stood in the doorway, turning her head from side to side.

Jessie didn't speak; she walked back and sat down again. She picked up the red book and stared at the picture, which represented a caterpillar, seated on a toadstool, blowing smoke from a large black hookah, while a tiny Alice faced him below the toadstool's rim.

Cora came, with a slight scowl; she had got cross pounding on the door. But the red book seemed to touch a fuzz of recollection. She came up and looked over Jessie's elbow.

"Daddy read you this," said Jessie, staring at the child full-on. "Remember, Cora? Last night? About Alice. About *Alice*."

The sea-blue eye, set wide, regarded her without a flicker of interest. Their faces were close; it was as though Jessie had never seen Cora so distinctly.

"She *ate* the *mushroom*," said Jessie in a low clear voice. "She *ate* it all up. To get *bigger* and *smaller*. Remember? Remember how she *ate* the mushroom and *grew*? Daddy read you."

This was within Cora's power. Her eyes left Jessie's face and fastened on the confusing picture. The short blunt finger came up hesitantly and touched the glazed image and drew back, dissatisfied, from its texture. She lifted her eyes and fastened them instead on Jessie.

"I saw it!" said Jessie, and she smiled radiantly at the child. "I *saw* the mushroom, the one that made her *bigger* and *smaller*. It's here, it's right *here*. At the top of the glen, near the rock."

There was silence, in which the dog barked again, distantly; he must be chained. Cora still looked at her with a wide absence, but her brows were drawn together. Jessie could hear her own voice, light and sure as a smile, caressing Cora. "The *mushroom* Alice *ate*!" she cried triumphantly. A quick squint contracted Cora's lids, her eyes darkened slightly. She turned them to the book, but then quickly back to Jessie. "It's by the rock, just at the top of the glen. The mushroom Alice ate. And grew smaller. And bigger."

They stared at each other for a minute. Then Cora contracted the muscles of her throat in an almost soundless tiny roar. She swung around, and Jessie, motionless as the transfixed squirrel, watched her to the screen door, which she opened. Then she stopped and turned around, glaring in confusion; but Jessie gave her a clear, secure smile. At that she contracted her lids and suddenly stretched back the corners of her mouth—it was almost a smile. It was, a kind of smile. She stood, big against the light, rocking slightly in a tremendous excitement. Then she stepped carefully down onto the grass and the screen door slammed behind her.

For a minute Jessie did not get up, and by the time she silently shut the wood door and went to the window, Cora was stumping with her ugly rocking walk across the lawn. It would take her minutes to get to the lip of the glen, and it was quite possible she might forget what she had come for.

With the door shut on the morning, the house seemed cold. Harmon had laid logs for tonight and there were paper and twigs below them. Jessie struck a match and stood, a little crouched, before the hearth, and sure enough, there came the stealing orange, flowing upward in a liquid mesh of flame, over the rough brown bark. There was no sound anywhere. But now in the silent room the fire began to pop and crackle faintly.

The Grasshopper's Burden

Here was this school building in the town, holding young and old, this stone building that looked from the front like a great big head with flat skull of asphalt and gravel and face of an insect that might be eating up the young through its opening and closing mouth of doors; and across its forehead were written the words: "Dedicated to all high emprise, the building of good citizens of the world, the establishment of a community of minds and hearts, free men and women."

In this building and in its surrounding yards were many people, children and teachers—it was a world:

This was a rainy afternoon in Social Studies and Quella could not stand hearing again the story of Sam Houston read out by different people in the class. She was just waiting for two-thirty when she would get her pass to go to the auditorium where the May Fete in which she was a Royal Princess (and one of two elected by the whole school) would be practiced.

Miss Morris, who would never at any time in her life have been a Royal Princess, she was so ordinary, was the Social Studies teacher and listening as she sat in good posture at her desk to the story of Sam Houston as if it were a brand-new tale just being told for the first time. She did not like to sign a pass—for anything, May Fetes included. Miss Morris had a puckered mouth just like a purse drawn up. She knew everything about children, whether they told a story about undone homework; and especially about boys, if they had been smoking or had a jawbreaker hidden over their last tooth, or a beanshooter in their blouse—she surmised a beanshooter so dreadfully that it might have been a revolver concealed there. And when she fussed at a boy who was mean by stealing a girl's purse and going through it, showing all a girl's things to other boys in the class, Miss Morris would draw her pursy mouth so tight that she seemed to have no lips at all and stitches would crack the powder around it. Then she would shake this boy hard, often causing bubblegum or jawbreakers to fall from him everywhere and roll hard on the floor under all the seats. She did not like to sign a pass.

But Quella must have an early pass, not only to keep from having to read her turn at Sam Houston but to give her time to go get her hair ready for the May Fete practice. She thought what an early pass might be for— not to go to the Nurse to see if she had mumps because it felt sore by her

Reprinted with permission from *Ghost and Flesh: Stories and Tales* by William Goyen (Random House, 1952); copyright © by William Goyen.

ear, because yesterday she had said this and caused a lot of attention, but all the M's in her row and the L's and N's on both sides of her row shrank away from her and even Helena McWorthy had not wanted to go around with her between classes, the way they did, seeing what was in the halls together, or let her use her powder puff or blue woman's comb, just to get mumps. And she could not have something in her eye because not long ago she had got an easy pass from Miss Stover in Math for this and the Nurse, a little mean woman that smelled like white, had said, "I find nothing whatsomever in your eye that does not naturally belong there," and wrote this on a note to Miss Stover and then glared at her with the whites of her eyes.

Quella sneaked a good black jawbreaker into her mouth, acting like she was just brushing her hand across her mouth, and Miss Morris never knew. Then she sat, waiting for a reason to get an early pass to dawn upon her. She could hear the voices of this one and that one reading out about Sam Houston—forever Sam Houston! They had had him in the Third Grade and they had had him in the Fifth. And now, even in the Seventh and as far as Junior High School they had to have him again. It was Mable Sampson, the biggest girl, reading now. If she would say *thee—ee*, Miss Morris would stop her and make her say it *thuh*; and she could not even pronounce the word that clearly spelled *Puritan* but said it *Prutan*. Mabel Sampson was so dumb. Because Mabel Sampson was bigger than the rest of the class, she deviled them and snooted them whenever and wherever she could, to make it plain that she had somewhere (and Quella was going to find out) passed all the rest of them on her way to something and would get there first.

And then it was Billy Mangus reading. He was fat and white and whined a lot, and the worst boy to sit in front of if you were a girl and an M. She and Helena McWorthy just hated him for what he would do with redhots. He would plant these little dots of sticky candy in Helena McWorthy's beautiful hair and she would not even know it or feel them there and go all through the halls between classes having redhots in her hair until someone laughed at her and made fun of her and picked them out to eat them. Or Billy Mangus would bore a sharpened pencil into Helena's back right through an Angora sweater or even her Mexican bolero which her aunt brought her back from Tijuana, Mexico. Helena was a very quiet girl. She would let Quella stroke her, huddled blinking in her seat, keep her always right and everything about her straight, plait and unplait and plait again her hair, arrange her ribbons. Helena would go anywhere holding Quella's hand, submissive to be with her. She had little chinkapin eyes fixed close to the bridge of her nose like a cheap doll's, dull and with scant white eyebrows. Her almost white hair, which was long and divided down her back, was infested with lures like sometimes two red plastic butterflies lighted there, or a green Spanish comb staked over one ear, and always red or blue knitting yarn wound through a spliced hawser of it, which arched over the top of her head from ear to ear. Helena had discovered that a pencil, too, might be stuck there and stolen often by Billy Mangus, who sat behind her alphabetically, and have to be fussed for.

Billy Mangus was reading and Quella wondered if his false tooth in front was wiggling, and she stretched over to see. No. It must be locked in place now. But if he wanted to, Billy could, by unlocking this false tooth some way with his tongue, cause it to wiggle like a loose picket in a fence. This tooth was his special thing in a class or anywhere if he wanted to unlock it. Suddenly she just had to see it wiggle and she did not know why but she shouted, right in the middle of the reading, "Wiggle us your tooth, Billy!" This made Miss Morris very outdone and Billy Mangus giggled and the whole class tittered. Miss Morris made everything quiet, then stared so hard at Quella and all the class sat very still to watch Miss Morris do one of her stares, hold her rocky eyes, never even breathing or blinking, right on a pupil until he had to look down first. Quella did not know whether to try to outstare Miss Morris by doing just the same to her until *she* put her eyes down, or to look to see if Billy Mangus was wiggling his tooth. But she decided she would rather see the tooth and turned to look; and so Miss Morris won. "Sit up straight, Quella, and do not talk one more time out of turn!" Miss Morris said, very proud because she had won a staring contest.

Quella sat up in her seat and there seemed nothing to do, so she remembered her lips, if they had enough lipstick on them. Very carefully she opened her nice black patent-leather purse and got out her lady's mirror which was of red-skinned leather and had some redhots sticking to it. She cleaned them off into her purse to save them and held out the mirror for her lips to see themselves. She put her lips in a round soft circle. She saw them in her mirror, red enough, sweetheart lips, so beautiful. Then she made different shapes with them, some kissing shapes, some like "OOOOO!"; and one like being prissy, or a word like "really!"; or like the Nurse saying "I find nothing whatsomever in your eye that does not naturally belong there." But she would not do her lips like Miss Morris at a mean boy, for then it would spoil the lipstick. Last, she gently kissed a piece of composition paper to leave her lips there. Liz her sister kissed letters at the end and all over, she mailed her lips to boys, and she would, too, when she began to write letters to somebody besides her Grandmother in Yreka, who would certainly not be thrilled with kissing lips in a letter.

Then she put her mirror back in her purse and spied her big blue comb in there. She scraped some redhots off it and brought it out and raked her hair with it. It was a good feeling. She thought of Helena's bunch of hair and how she wanted right now to be behind her plaiting it and fixing it as she did in Science where they did not have to sit alphabetically. She seined her hair again through the net of her comb, right in back this time, being very careful not to comb down the red ribbon which was pinned there like an award for something. If a boy pulled at it, this would make her mad and stamp her foot and have to slap him. She lolled the black jawbreaker around in her mouth and devoured the sweet juice from it.

Then suddenly there was something being unwrapped cunningly in the L's across from her. She looked to see Charlotte Langendorf, the ugliest girl, holding something sticky and blue in her lap. It had been wrapped in wax paper. "What is that stuff?" she whispered across to Charlotte. "A thing we cooked today in Cooking and I am going to eat it when the eating period comes," Charlotte whispered, glad someone had noticed it. "Let me see it," Quella whispered again. "I won't eat it, cross my heart. I have Cooking next period and I need to know what we will cook." Charlotte passed it secretly across and Quella looked at this peculiar thing which they would cook next period. She examined it, smelled of it, and wanted right then to taste some of it. "What is it?" she asked. "It smells funny." "I don't know," Charlotte whispered back, "but it's something we made out of ingredients. Miss Starnes told us how." Quella tasted it. It was not good to eat at all, not even cooked; but she had another taste. "Let me have it!" Charlotte whispered severely. "Give me back my cooking!" Quella gave it back. "It smells tacky," she said. Then she looked ahead of her in the front of the S's and watched Bobby Sandro's broken arm in a cast, how he was writing tattoos on it, in a cast and a sling from breaking it in Gym and he did not have to write because of it. And then at Suzanne Prince's bandaged-up finger, so she couldn't write, too, saying it was bitten by their cat that went insane.

And then she surveyed the whole row of mean boys, every one of them mean, not a one cute, whose names began with B as though all the meanest were named alike, and she thought how they would step on your saddle shoes to dirty them. Then she thought of several things in a row: horses and their good gentle one named Beauty they used to have; of a fight in the rain before school by Joe and Sandy and how all the girls stood purposely to get their hair wet and be so worried about it; of Liz and her boy friend Luke Shimmens who owned a hot-rod and took them riding around town and up and down dragging Main blowing the horn and backfiring and seeing different kids walking along and waving out at them.

Then there seemed nothing else going on to see or do, and Quella wanted to have an early pass again. Wayne Jinks was just finishing his paragraph. When it was over she raised her hand and popped it to jingle the jingles round her wrist. Miss Morris said, "Do you want to read next, Quella?" "Nome," Quella said, and prissed, "it is time to go to May Fete practice."

Miss Morris said a surprise. "All right, take a pass and go ahead." And she took a pad of passes from her drawer and wrote on one. She tore it off and gave it to Quella, looking for a moment as if she were going to stare at her. But Quella went out of the room quickly.

She was in the hall with a pass in her hand, going down the very quiet hall that did not have another single person in it. She passed all the rooms, sometimes seeing through a door pane some teacher writing on a blackboard or standing talking to a class. She noticed as she went along that without any other kids, alone in the hall (and this same thing was true when she was by herself with a teacher), she was no more than somebody quiet and courteous. But when the others were around, she could be all the things they were, shouting and slapping boys and eating at the wrong time, provoked with the way things were or excited about them. She stopped by the closed door to the Teachers' Room where all their mailboxes were, like pigeons' holes. No one was in there. She remembered seeing the teachers gathered in front of their boxes before the first class began, fumbling, dipping and rising like homing pigeons. She came by Miss Purlow's room where the Stuttering Class was—in there was George Kurunus and she spied him through the glass pane of the door, sitting like some kind of an animal. She heard Miss Purlow's perfect words, like "lit-tle," like "yel-low" floating across the room, how she would say every word right. And next was Mrs. Stanford, who would treat you so very nice when you met her in the grocery store after school, or on Saturdays, with her hand on your head, saying, "How's little Quella?" and patting you, but mean in class and acting as though she never had seen you in a grocery store in her life, or anywhere. Then here was the typing class. It was like a heavy rain in there. And old Miss Cross, who had been teaching how to type for thirty years, standing at the front of the class pointing with a long stick at the letters on a chart and saying "A" and then an enormous clack! to make an A, then "B" and another clack to make this letter. Then faster, and it was like a slow gallop of a horse on pavement and Miss Cross with her stick like a circus trainer, "A - S - D - F - G." And next was Miss Winnie's room where this teacher cried a lot and for this was called Weeping Winnie and spoke in a soft cooing voice and seemed so sad. She always lost her voice the Ninth Period and said, "Cheeldrin you will have to write today, my voice is gone."

As she went along she would walk like different kinds of people, or in different ways, very quickly and hopping; or as she had seen Miss Mc-

Murray, the English teacher and very pretty, going down the halls—as though she were carrying a bag of eggs, afraid to break them, or a sleeping baby that might be waked; and like the Royal Princess with a train that she had been voted to be in the May Fete. Then she meandered in big S's or in zig-zags from one side of the hall to the other; or smeared one finger along the wall, loitering, browsing, lolling at every drinking fountain to sip a long time or spew the water back. She saw some faded redhots and the little stone of a jawbreaker in one fountain.

Once she thought of Helena and wished Helena could be with her. Helena was such a beautiful name. She came to her sister Liz's room and peeked in. The good-looking Mr. Forbes was teaching them some important senior subject and they were all listening as if what he was saying had to be learned to take out in the world when they would soon go. She looked to see what color his tie was today. Liz had counted seventeen different ties in seventeen days on Mr. Forbes and he wore so many different kinds of coats and trousers that they said he changed sometimes between classes. Yes, he had his saddle shoes on, too. Then she saw Mr. Forbes looking towards the door where she was. She ducked down quickly to wait until he turned and she could look again for Liz, to see how she looked sitting up in class.

As she crouched there she suddenly heard someone coming down the hall and looked to see who could it be. It was the awful deformity George Kurunus writhing and slobbering and skulking towards her. She was afraid of him and thought she would scream as all the girls did when he came to them; but she knew if you went up to him not afraid of his twisted face and said George to him and talked to him he would not do anything to you. Together, all the kids played with him, at him, as though he was some crazy and funny thing like a bent toy on a string; but no one ever wanted to be with him alone. Often a class would hear a scratching at the door and would see his hoodlum face at a door pane like Hallowe'en and be frightened until they saw it was just George Kurunus. Then the class would laugh and make faces back at him and the teacher would go to the door and say "Now, George . . ." and shoo him away; and the class would titter. The boys all went around with him as if he was something they owned, something they could use for some stunt or trick on somebody, their arms around his shoulder; and they talked and laughed with him and told him ugly jokes and things about girls and sicked him on certain girls. Why did this deformity George have to be in a school? He couldn't even hold a word still in his mouth when he said it, for it rattled or hopped away—this was why he was in Stuttering Class, but it did him no good, he still broke a word when he said it, as if it were a twig, he still said ruined words.

He could not speak a word right and whole no matter how hard he tried or how carefully. But if you live among breakage, he may have reasoned, you finally see the wisdom in pieces; and no one can keep you from the pasting and joining together of bits to make the mind's own whole. What can break anything set back whole upon a shelf in the mind, like a mended dish? His mind, then, was full of mended words, broken by his own speech but repaired by his silences and put back into his mind. The wisdom in all things, in time, tells a meaning to those things, even to parcels of things that seem to mean disuse and no use, like scraps in a mending basket that are tokens and remnants of many splendid dresses and robes each with a whole to tell about.

Whenever the Twirling Class for girls in the Black and Gold Battalion practiced on the football field, here was this George on the field, too, like some old stray dog that had to be shooed away. And in a marching line of some class to somewhere, the library or a program in the auditorium, he ruined any straight marching line and so was put last to keep the line straight. But at the end of a straight marching line he twisted and wavered like the raveling out of a line and ruined it, even then; he was the capricious conclusion and mocking collapse of something all ordered and precise right up to the tag end. When he walked, it seemed he always ran upon himself like someone in the way—or like a wounded insect. He was a flaw in the school, as if he were a crack in the building.

This day he had sat in his row by the window and the sun was coming in upon him. It warmed his vestigial hand, lay upon a page of his book. It touched some leaves of a begonia on the teacher's desk and showed their white lines and illuminated the blooms to like glass flowers. *Flower* was a word, but he could not say it. The sun came in and lay upon Miss Purlow's face and showed where the round spot of rouge ended and her face's real skin began. The sun made, also, between Miss Purlow and the blackboard, a little transparent ladder leading up and out through the window. Specks of golden dust were popping in it, dancing and whirling on out the window. Then suddenly Miss Purlow walked through it and broke it, but it joined together again, in spite of Miss Purlow, and made him glad. Miss Purlow went to the blackboard and wrote upon it some perfectly shaped words in her pretty curlimacue handwriting that said:

> "*Come into the garden, Maud,*
> *For the black bat, night, has flown . . .*"

Then she read them aloud, musically and perfectly, and he so wanted to have these words in his mouth. Miss Purlow asked him to say them after her but he could not, they fell away from him, they were all hers; yet he had it perfect, the little melodious collection of words, in his mind from Miss Purlow's mouth, a small tune of sounds that hung clear and warbling in his ears like birdsong. He turned and shuffled away, to leave the room. Miss Purlow called at him that she would report him to the Principal again as soon as the class was over, but he did not care, he opened the door and went away from this room where he could not speak and where words tormented him.

Then here he was, ruining a quiet hall for Quella. Although with other children she laughed at him and thought him a funny thing, alone she was afraid of him and detested him. Where was this George going? He was shuffling closer. She stood up and pressed against the wall and watched him, hating him. It was said that if he ever fell down he could never get up unless somebody helped him, but just lie there scrambling and waving his arms and legs, like a bug on its back, and muttering. His little withered left arm was folded like a plucked bird's wing and its bleached and shriveled hand, looking as though it had been too long in water, was bent over and it hung limp like a dead fowl's neck and dangling head. But he could use this piece of hand, this scrap of arm quickly and he could snap it like a little quirt and pop girls as they passed him in the hall. Here he came, this crazy George Kurunus, a piece of wreckage in the school. What did *he* want? She looked to see if *he* had a pass in his hand. No. Certainly he was not going to practice for any May Fete. Why should *he* be in the halls and without a pass?

She shrank close to the wall, but did not want to be caught there by him. She decided to run fast past him, not looking at his goblin face and not going close enough to him to be popped by his whip of an arm. She darted and fled past him, wanting to push him down and leave him wriggling there in the hall. He said some sound, all drunken and garbled, to her as she passed him; but he did not try to pop her. She ran looking back at him and when she came to the turn of the hall that led to the lavatory, she ran around it fast, then crept back to peek around and see if he was still going on or coming after her. George Kurunus was staggering along, his knees scraping each other, sounding like a little puffing train in the hall, without ever looking back. This made her furious and she was going to yell, "Stuck u-up!" until she remembered she would be heard and was supposed to be going to the auditorium.

She ran into the girls' lavatory and was dramatically hiding from him there, panting faster than she really had to. She stopped to listen and heard his *sh-sh-sh-sh* down the hall away from her. This was another narrow escape she would tell Helena McWorthy about.

Then it was time for the May Fete practice and she went to the auditorium that always seemed so cool when the whole school wasn't in it. There were the royalty, already assembled: Joe Wright, the handsome King, also the Chief Yell Leader; Marveen Soames, the beautiful Queen, the other Princess, Hazel May Young, not pretty but with personality, and all the Dukes and Duchesses. Miss McMurray, the perfect-walking English teacher, was there to take charge.

They all marched down the aisle, very proud, and the King and Queen mounted the throne, the Princesses and Princes, Dukes and Duchesses swaggered to their places around the throne. The King had on his silver crown and was holding his tinfoil wand. When it was time to crown the Queen, the biggest moment of all, and everything was real quiet, all the empty seats in the auditorium hushed and watching, she spied in the glass frame of the auditorium door the terrible face of George Kurunus, like a grasshopper's face. He was watching the May Fete and had it all in his eye. This George Kurunus was everywhere, why did he have to be everywhere she was? But she turned her eyes away from him, upon all the beautiful royalty, and they went on with the practice. Then suddenly it was the bell for the next class, which was Homemaking—a dreary place for a Princess to go: to a cookstove after a coronation.

The Homemaking teacher was Miss Starnes and there she was, waiting for the girls at the door, smiling and standing straight. Miss Starnes would stand before her class reading from some book. Each day she had a fresh rose or some other flower from her own garden stuck to her strict dress, and the way she maneuvered her mouth and bowed and leaned her head towards the girls sitting before her made them know that she knew she was saying something good, as though she were smacking her lips and golloping something like a dessert. Yet Miss Starnes was very serious and meant what she would say or read and paused often, sticking out her chin (which had hairs on it) for emphasis.

The girls in Homemaking class who sat before her were not sure at all what these words meant, but they sat there, among the linen dresses and the fancy aprons hanging on hangers, which last year's class had made with its own hands and left the prices pinned on to show that they were good enough to be bought in any store. Then there was a manikin on a stand—in a corner by the American flag which the manikin seemed to need to drape around itself to hide its nakedness, headless and with a pole running right up through her to be her one leg; and in an adjoining room—the kitchen—there were rows of little stoves where Miss Starnes told the girls things to cook.

The bell had rung and all the girls were in their seats—any chosen seat and not alphabetically—and "responsibility" was a word Miss Starnes was already smacking off her lips to the girls in Homemaking. "Domestic respon-si-bi-li-ty." These were words Miss Starnes started right in telling to the class, things they should be or do in the good home they would have or make—and which lay off somewhere in the vague unknown and which they could not quite see as something of theirs but just imagine and did not even particularly want, now. But whatever or wherever or however

this place "The Home," they would be there, all these girls, going indus-
triously around in aprons, there would be a lot of busy sewing and a
difficult cooking, and . . . "Domestic re-spon-si-bi-li-ty" . . . these words
Miss Starnes was saying.

Quella was going to start in plaiting and unplaiting Helena McWorthy's hair when Miss Starnes kneaded and worked her lips and they were
getting ready to say another careful word to the class. "E-con-o-my." The
manikin was standing there in the corner trying to be that word, which
was a good thing to be. The manikin was a pitiful thing, undressed, or
something headless like a fowl, or something deformed, but proud and
seeming to want to help Miss Starnes with the lecture by standing there
as though it, too, were teaching Homemaking. It was about the size of her
mother in her short slip in the summertime, Quella observed.

And then Miss Starnes led them in the kitchen and they were going
to cook their lesson. "I know what it will be," Quella told the others.
"Like some stuff Charlotte Langendorf cooked first period and carried in
wax paper to Social Studies—of potatoes or something." But Miss Starnes
was saying that in this class today there would be cooked pudding and to
light the stoves and listen to some things she would say about the making
of pudding, and to put on their white cook aprons. "Ingredients" was a
word about pudding which Miss Starnes was saying, and it seemed just
the word for what milk and sugar, which they were already mixing,
looked like together. There was a gregarious stirring. Then Miss Starnes
told about the soft ball that the mixture would make in a cup of cold
water to show it was ready. Here and there already a soft ball was found
in a cup and a girl would raise her hand to tell it to Miss Starnes.

Just as Quella's and Helena's mixture made a soft ball for them in
their cup of cold water, a staccato bell-ringing that was certainly not the
regular bell resounded in the school building, and it was fire drill. Although the mixture was ready and showed its undeniable sign, all the
Homemaking girls had to leave it and line up in two's and march behind
Miss Starnes through the hall smelling of their mixture which even then,
though it was not yet anything but ingredients, made them feel important
because they had caused this smell to move all in the corridors just as
they were moving now, and even reach around as far as the algebra room,
where there were no good smells, and hang under the noses of the class
doing unknowns. The girls marched and fretted.

When the Homemaking class got outside under the trees where the
school busses were waiting for school to be out, and stood in their right
place under the cottonwood trees, Miss Starnes suddenly thought about
the windows in Homemaking and remembered she had not closed and
locked them according to fire drill instructions. "Quella," she said carefully as though she were saying "do-mes-tic" or "e-con-o-my," "please to

run back to Homemaking and close all the windows tight and see that no stoves are burning."

"Don't I need a pass?" Quella asked.

"No, Quella. Run."

She was alone in the hall again. The pudding will be ruined, she thought. If the school burns, they will have to save the pudding and the May Fete pretties. She could smell smoke, and then once she was sure she saw a flame lick out of Boys' Lavatory, but she would never go in *there* to put it out. She went very fast to Homemaking and in the room she went right to her and Helena's cup with the soft ball in it. She felt it. It was still soft. She went around looking at other cups. Margy Reynolds' was not ready but was still just ingredients in a cup of water. But some hand or finger had been in it all, in all the cups and pans, who had been meddling in Homemaking? She thought she heard the crackling of flames above her, so she rushed to close the windows, and as she ran out, she swiped her finger through her and Helena's ready mixture and strung it along the stove and floor and on her dress; but she licked it up quick and slammed the door.

Then she ran through the hall, not liking the halls this way, with no pass, without classes in the rooms, no different teachers standing or sitting there as she passed them. How scarey the school seemed now, full of the echoes of her clapping feet and her panting. She passed Miss Purlow's room and looked in through the door. On the blackboard were written the lines in beautiful penmanship:

"*Come into the garden, Maud,*
For the black bat, night, has flown . . ."

and under the lines was—what? Was it a joke or what? There was a curious disheveled chaos of giant and dwarf runaway shapes, tumbled and humped and crazy . . . like the Devil's writing or like a ghost's. She ran.

Then she was by the auditorium and stopped to make sure there was no flame in there to eat up all the May Fete pretties—the dresses and the paper flowers, the paper wand and all the paper streamers. She could feel something in there! There was some live thing in there! She listened. No sound. She looked through the pane of the auditorium door and what should she spy but George Kurunus sitting on the King's Throne like a crazy king in a burning building. On his head was the silver crown and in his ruined hand the silver wand. He was into everything, who would keep him out of all the things at school; he was a disturbance in this world of school and in her own world, touching and tampering with everything she did. She thought she saw him rise and come down from the throne and down the aisle towards her, after her; and she ran away and down the hall, now full of smoke she was sure, hearing him after her—*sh-sh-sh-sh*—and seeing rags of flame waving out from alcoves and recesses at her. She ran out the door and into the open, without looking back. If the schoolhouse burned it would burn him like a cricket in it. She would not tell.

She was thrilled to see all the boys and all the girls lined under the trees and gladly joined them. She stood shivering under the trees in her place in line, waiting to see what was going to happen, in the unearthly quiet that lay over all the school people, over all the school building. Suddenly at a window on the second floor she saw his face, as if her fear of fire had a face and it was George Kurunus'. No one else seemed to see it— was she imagining it? for she now had the insect-headed and devil-bodied image of him in her head. No, there it was, his face, looking down at her, she was sure. And then she thought she saw him crying! If he was crying she wanted to save him from the burning building, to call out that he was in there, or to run in and save him herself; hurry! hurry! hurry! But suddenly the all-clear bell that would bring them all back to where he was, separate and waiting, but never back to him whirred out, convulsing through her whole body and through his own tilted body like electric shock . . . it was all a nightmare: if there had been no fire then there had been no George in the empty building, she thought.

Now they all began to move, in their colors like a field of flowers jostling in the wind; and she saw again, for sure, his grasshopper face at the window, watching them coming back to the skulled building of stone that held him like an appetite or a desire that would surely, one day, get them every one: all the beautiful schoolchildren gathered and moving like the chosen through the heavenly amber afternoon light and under the golden leaves—the lean ball-players, the agile jitterbuggers, the leaping perch of yell leaders, the golden-tongued winners of the declamation contests, Princes and Princesses, Duchesses and Kings, and she, Quella, among them, no safer than the rest but knowing, at least, one thing more than the rest.

The Sacrifice

There is a tradition among the Basques, varying with the locality, but practiced still in remote hamlets. It is pagan. At the harvest, a festival is held, lasting as long as a week. Wild pigeons are netted, sometimes by the thousands. There is a stock fair. Teams of oxen compete pulling sledges weighted with boulders. A bowling championship is held, there are sometimes scratch jai-alai matches, and soccer games. Every evening there is dancing, and at midnight fireworks.

Itinerant carnivals roll into town. Booths are set up. Men and boys plink with air rifles at threads from which caramels are suspended. Children fish in troughs for trinkets, using little wooden lollipop sticks with twine and a hook. There are all sorts of rides: the merry-go-round with prancing steeds impaled on candy striped poles; the Ferris wheel. Mellifluous barkers cadge women into the purchase of ribbons and combs, showing off an innumerable variety of tin openers and potato peelers that are magical in the hands of the demonstrator but never work at home. The men are all half tipsy; the women (in Jacobo's time) are dressed in their gorgeous and elaborate provincial costumes, with white cotton leggings, long and copious velvet skirts in scarlet, blue, or green, squeezed as tight as respiration will allow at the waist, and topped by equally tight but modest bodices that are heavily embroidered.

The festivities are opened in the central town square by officials of the Ayuntamiento, all looking flushed and portentous. If the town is important enough, an ecclesiastical dignitary—perhaps even a bishop—will celebrate solemn High Mass, assisted by the local curate and a bevy of red-surpliced boys. From the surrounding hills come farmers and their families, who, during most of the year, live virtually isolated, driving their little milk wagons and towing cattle for display, trade, or sale.

The last day, the local saint's day, the day of the High Mass, is the climax. That is when the "king" of the festival meets his fate. All week long he has been paraded in a brightly painted cart drawn by a pair of white mules whose headbands and tails are braided with red geraniums, his royal way prepared by a court of the fairest lasses and the most stalwart lads. His scepter is a bullrush, wreathed with the tassels of maize. His crown is a garland of marigold, and his hair has been sprinkled with the scales of sardines, so that it shines all silver and blue. For seven days, sweets and delicacies have been stuffed into his mouth. He has merely to nod for a mug of frothing cider to be thrust at him, and wherever he passes, people bow low, pelting him with nosegays—laughing boisterously the while. Because it is one of the village idiots who is chosen to reign.

In the autumn of 1935, this lot fell to Salvador Ybarra. There was no one except possibly the vet to distinguish between mongolism and cerebral palsy. The selection was by ballot. It was irreversible. No help that Salvador was a nephew once removed of José Ybarra, the mayor: Sacedón was poor in idiots that year, the new generation had produced fewer, and it was law that no king reigned twice. Marisol wept when the horseman in plumed black cavalier's hat and a swirling black cape galloped up to the homestead, rearing the white-eyed pony back on its shaggy heels as he cast the proclamation onto the mud of the stoop, reining hard about and galloping back down the mountain. She could not bear to look into her brother's eyes, which were ringed with fright and horror, because he knew all about the feast and the honor and what would happen to him. When Jacobo, later on that afternoon, heard, his heart—by far the largest muscle in his body—almost burst. He went pounding up the hills to the Ybarra cottage. One glance at Marisol, and a glance at Salvador . . . Uninvited, he intruded into the cottage, to find mother and father sitting near the hearth, heads bent in anguish and resignation. "Hide him!" Jacobo cried. "Let me take him into the hills and hide him!" They thanked the young man, Rivas that he is, but they shook their heads. It was the Custom. Custom was not to be denied.

All that week, Salvador presided. He managed his office with unwonted poise, ignoring cheers and jeers as he garlanded the team of winning oxen and handed prizes to the owners of the champion cow or bull or hog. Summoning what must have been a tremendous force from within, he managed to subdue most of his facial contortions. He drooled only every now and then, although whenever to the delight of the children, whose peals of merriment and pointing fingers he seemed not to mind. Day by day, however, the terror masked behind his eyes mounted; and Jacobo, watching, felt his tendons swell and blood go rushing into his brain. As much as possible, he stayed away from the festivities, forfeiting his chance of dancing with Marisol; who, of course, whatever she felt, had to take part. Nothing could forestall, abridge, or abrogate the rites. From beginning to end, they were observed.

At sundown on the last day, Salvador was escorted to the town square. In front of the Ayuntamiento and across from the church, carpenters had hammered together a platform. It was in the form of a squat, flat-topped Roman bridge, with a landing to the rear for Salvador's throne. The structure was festooned with autumnal blossoms. It was hung with the fruits of the season: ripe red tomatoes on their stalks, plump pumpkins, leathery long-necked calabashes, mottled green melons, and large, round, luscious-looking apples. With all decorum, Salvador was seated. His court, after sprinkling him with flower petals, withdrew, dividing by sex down the stairs and posting themselves at the foot of the dais like sentinels. Salvador was looking very pale, now. He had begun to tremble, and his limbs to twitch. More than 2,000 souls had assembled. He looked down on 2,000 ruddy, smiling faces. The great bronze bells of the church tower began clamoring. One by one, led by the agintari, women and men, young and old, trooped up the stairs from the left, reached the landing, bent their right knee to Salvador, and then proceeded down the flight of stairs to the right. Not until the last person had paid homage did the bells cease tolling. There was silence. A river of expectation ran through the crowd, and a rumble of talk that grew and grew. Then, suddenly, at a signal, rockets streamed into the purple sky, exploding with hollow booms and showering the canopy with brilliant gold, silver, red and blue sparks. Battery after battery went up, in a gorgeous display, extruding gasps of admiration from 2,000 throats. Night fell with a clap.

All grew still. Above, bats and martins swooped. From the belfry, pigeons cooed. Little more than a murmur emanated from the crowd. Necks were craned to the balustrade of the town hall, above Salvador, where the council had gathered. José Ybarra, sweeping the multitude with his eyes, then glancing at the old curate (who smacked at the wax clogging his good ear in conformity), let a white handkerchief flap over the railing.

Salvador shrieked. His cry was scattered into atoms by the roar of the crowd. All surged forward. In mock panic, the king's court fled. Shouting, a pack of burly youths raced for the stairs of the dais, people massing and pressing behind them. Two reached the landing at just about the same time. Arms raised, they lunged at a Salvador now rigid in his sacrificial seat.

And that was when it happened. Skulking underneath the platform throughout the ceremony had been Jacobo. He had heard the boom of the last rocket; he had endured he knew not how the heart-stopping silence that followed; and he had felt to his marrow the famished bestial growl erupting on the signal of the white handkerchief. Lifting his hands to the rear edge of the platform, he swung himself up. At the very moment of the lunge of the two youths, Jacobo came at them from behind the throne, bulling them back against their fellows.

Everybody halted. There, in command of the landing, covering Salvador, Jacobo stood. He seemed to have reared up from nowhere, feet planted ten inches apart, oaken legs rooted—calling out of a strangled throat, "*Don't anybody try . . . Don't one of you touch him!*"

The shock of this rupture in ritual lasted moments. Salvador, behind

Jacobo, struggled with his tongue, urging, "Go, g-go, they'll k-k-k-kill you!" Because the king had to be sacrificed, his crown torn off, his scepter dashed to the ground, his face spat upon, and his writhing body dragged through the multitude to be reviled and pelted by dung and kicked and slapped and finally dumped atop the other garbage of an abandoned quarry. Next year's crops depended on it. But the young men on the flights of stairs to Jacobo's left and right did not move. Below him, the crowd gawked. From above, mouths agape, hung the astonished heads of the town's council. The stench of cordite was thick in everyone's nostrils.

Then, from somewhere in the middle ranks of the mob came a long, quavering, "You ninny, get down from there!" It was Manú Rivas, mortified. His voiced seemed to wake José Ybarra out of a daze, and he called from the gallery, "Jacobo, don't be foolish!" But Jacobo seemed deaf, his great chest heaving, mouth, nostrils, and eye sockets black hollows on a broad pale face. "Do what must be done!" José Ybarra ordered the youths on the stairs. They responded with a tentative advance, recoiling at once as Jacobo, come alive, dealt a massive stamp on the boards of the platform and bawled at them, "*No! Leave him free!*"

But he was no leader of men. There was appeal in this cry, mighty though the lungpower impelling it. Jacobo was rushed from both sides. A thickset butcher's son was first to reach him. Jacobo plucked the fellow up in his huge arms and hurled him into the faces of those below. The next four he grabbed and disposed of in similar fashion, and there was at least one crack of a collarbone. The people yelled in a crescendo of outrage. Above them all the voice of Manú Rivas pierced, shrilling obscenities. Now hordes of hardy peasants, young and middle-aged, went crowding up both flights of stairs. Jacobo was a bear, ferocious, looming above a pack of wolves, but they were too many. A club landed on his skull. He shuddered, buckling. With cries of rage and vengeance, his attackers swarmed over him. The man with the club raised it once more, high: and himself fell stunned to the floor of the landing.

The yokes used in the north of Spain are blocked out of dense pine. A yoke may weight fifteen or more pounds. The yoke that landed on the head of Jacobo's attacker weighed at least that, and it was wielded by Marisol Ybarra. She had followed Jacobo's initiative, working her way under the dais and clambering up from behind. She had been followed by Amadeo, who was gloriously drunk, who pushed the yoke onto the platform after her and then struggled aboard himself, each hand armed with a fat wineskin. He swayed on the platform—behind the throne—rollicking with joy as he boffed the pig's bladders down on heads poking up from below. He was not seen by the people. It was Marisol who impressed them. She towered over most men. Under the torch lights, her black eyes flashed like gunpowder igniting. Her brawny arms bulged with muscle, and her bosom heaved with imperial and manifestly murderous emotion. With one sweep of her yoke, she cleared four men off the landing, fracturing a skull and smashing several teeth.

Her intervention gave Jacobo time to recover. He rose, shaking off an assailant who as much clutched at him for protection against Marisol as to fight. The moment she saw Jacobo on his feet, Marisol thrust the yoke at him. She stepped back. Amadeo thrust his wineskins into her hands. He contented himself with stamping on people's fingers and aiming kicks at their faces, simultaneously gathering tomatoes and calabashes and pumpkins and with rapturous howls lobbing them at anyone he saw. Jacobo dominated the center of the landing, using the yoke like a boom, in single swipes eliminating or knocking off their feet half a dozen or more men. Those who were not wholly put out of commission were sandbagged by Marisol, who also traveled from wing to wing of the dais and methodically repelled boarders.

Side by side and back to back the three fought. For a time, they had the advantage. The very numbers of the indignant crowd worked against them. But they were now coming from all sides. Amadeo was the first to fall, uttering a reproachful little clucking sound as a rock bounced off his forehead and he toppled like a trained gymnast over the edge of the platform and under the dais, where he snoozed in comfort and safety the rest of the night. Marisol was overpowered next: by her own father, who managed to noose her in a rope, dragging her off the platform with the help of fellow Ybarras, to whom this defiance of tradition was of particular shame. Jacobo lasted not many moments longer, downed by the swing of a wine bottle. He was kicked and trampled. Then over his body rushed the men, reaching the throne at last, where Salvador, clutching his scepter, sat without a muscle quavering. And it was consummated.

There were consequences to this affair. The "king" hanged himself that night from a beam in the family's shed, using tough wire twine that cut through muscle and bone, decapitating him. The Ybarras as a clan suffered a blow to their prestige, which should have comforted Manú, but which did not, because the blow Jacobo had dealt the Rivas name was irredeemable (Manú did not learn until some months later that Amadeo had participated in the outrage; by which time both were past caring, because Amadeo succumbed to hepatitis). Half dead, Jacobo was dragged back to the stable and dumped in the straw. He bled profusely from head, ears, nose, and mouth. Two ribs were broken. He could hardly breathe. The veterinarian presented himself at midnight. Manú bid him begone. But the vet, if not especially competent, was a kind man. He reminded

Manú that he had two cows fresh that might be needing professional assistance; and thus gained entrance to the stable, where he dressed Jacobo's wounds, stitched his scalp, finished removing a loose incisor, and bound his chest. It is likely, however, that this attention would have been unavailing, infection set in, and Jacobo died: because he was given no care at all by any member of his family except Amadeo, who did his best to pluck the maggots out of his brother's flesh.

An Unrung Bell

The disabled find life sweet like anyone else. "The missing legs / Of the amputee / Are away somewhere / Winning a secret race," says Phil Dacey in his poem "The Handicapped." In David Wagoner's mysterious poem "How Stump Stood in the Water," one feels that Stump does not mind being considered useless. Enough that he "stood alone / On his own feet, holding his life in his hands." The joy of sex is not denied the disabled, as testified by Richard Ronan in "Seated Nude," one of the most erotic poems ever written, regardless of the fact that it celebrates the prowess of a paralyzed man. Ronald Wallace celebrates his father's wild sense of freedom upon getting a chin-operated wheelchair after being paralyzed from the neck down for twenty years. The crippled beggar in Louis Simpson's poem "Stumpfoot on 42nd Street" enjoys unstrapping his apparatus and lighting a cigar. "These freaks are alive in earnest. / He is not embarrassed. / It is for you to feel embarrassed, / Or God, or the way things are." The hemophiliac in Hollis Summers' "Bleeder" takes his pleasure in teaching children with his problem at a summer camp. Even Happy in John Gilgun's story represents with his truculent independence a sort of triumph. He, too, along with all the handicapped in this last section, is "an unrung bell."

The Handicapped

1
The missing legs
Of the amputee
Are away somewhere
Winning a secret race.

2
The blind man has always stood
Before an enormous blackboard,
Waiting for the first
Scrawl of light,
That fine
Dusty chalk.

3
Here
The repetitions of the stutterer,
There
The flickering of the stars.

4
Master of illusion,
The paralytic alone moves.
All else is still.

5
At Creation,
God told the deaf,
"Only you will hear
The song of the stone."

6
Dare not ask
What the dumb
Have been told to keep secret.

7
When the epileptic
Falls in a fit,
He is ascending
To the heaven of earth.

How Stump Stood in the Water

Ice had many sons. "Find me my food!" he shouted.
They searched in the air and under the water
And brought him Quail and Mussel, Goose and Oyster,
Blue Teal and Rock Crab, Widgeon and Salmon.

"More! More!" Ice shouted. "My sons must feed me!"
Some climbed after Eagle and fell. Some paddled
After Gray Whale and drowned. Some offered
Buzzard and Minnow, Coot and Sea Slug.

But Stump stood in the ocean, catching nothing.
"Foolish Stump!" Ice shouted. "What are you standing on?
What are you holding in your shut hands?
Feed me! Feed me!" But Stump said, "Father,

What am I standing on? What am I holding?
If you tell me, they will be yours forever."
Ice shouted, "You are standing on Flounder!
You have stolen the last sweet eggs of Killdeer

For your selfish dinner! The tide is rising!
Who brings me nothing will come to nothing!"
Then Ice pulled back his other sons to the north,
And the water rose, and the water ebbed away.

And on the barren shore, Stump stood alone
On his own feet, holding his life in his hands.

Reprinted by permission of Indiana University Press from *Who Shall Be the Sun?* by David Wagoner;
copyright © 1978 by David Wagoner.

A Late Elegy for a Baseball Player

He was all back,
his stance was clumsy,
ran like a horse,
smiled with a dimple,
but Time cut him,
as easy as that,

bowled him right over,
muscle and all, for
a crick in his honest back—
the wellwrought stallion,
cleats on his shoes,
and a hometown shoulder,

full of country bumps.
We read about Herakles
and the hairy Samson,
and fake Olympic games:
the whole world boos—
but here's Big Lou

whom Death bowled over
as the sun rose,
a lazy foul ball,
and a whole generation
of the running boys
pull up, cry loud

at what Death caught.

Seated Nude

she hiked; knew she had to.
summer last she paced up the
eastern edge of canada; the year before
up the lower spine of the appalachian.
this year it was ireland in the
constant rain.
he understood; also knew that he had to.
he was a greatly hairy man,
smelling like a stale red fur; she
a fine, thin woman who'd become,
in two years, near-wild
with raw halves of beef, cattle storms,
fire and glacial till moving, scratching
across her inside flesh:
all love and rage. she was the first
to say it; she'd talked it all through.
he, too, had talked it through.
they had friends with ears, outlets
for the wobbling sense of futility,
for the moments when the need
to entertain decision reigned; friends
also for when it passed
and only grim circumstance sat
in its sparse corner. they talked through
all the elements, all the feelings
surrounding the elements: the confine
to the chair, his death from the torso
downward, her life tipped over, dragging
like an oak table caught on a leash,
his embarrassment at being baggage
to himself, to her—
they *knew* themselves and their situation.
it was no one's fault; there was no
apologizing for it; no anger at it—
—such retreat wasn't their province;
they couldn't even borrow it and be fair;
it was their simple *fact* that
they daily faced,

not their points-of-view, each leaning
in against the other,
not even their great regard
for each other—but fact,
circumstance: their life, unlike most,
became only itself.

he had been a good lover; had
matched her good mind and her good
bony body with a thick lust,
a good sense of who she was.
he'd been short; she taller.
in bed, he liked to climb her.
after the crippling, he did what tongue,
red beard and fingers could do
—and it was considerable, too.
he hauled the listless hips
with a kind of art across her bed,
such that her loss might be less
than the loss of a toy, a seven-inch bat.
it sufficed as distraction.
and through all this vast recompense,
he grew large muscles in the arms and
neck and face. the chest fattened; rose
into cakes. like a gymnast,
he swung his unresponding legs
through the house on a clever sequence
of rings and dance-bars
that he'd devised for himself.
he seldom fell; she seldom had
clear reason to weep
and the little deaths
of the heart and the large fall
of meaning in their life were, thus,
kept in stay, like two wars maintained
on either side of a wall.
still, one night, while she lay
opened to his face and fierce arms,
she knew suddenly—and it is sometimes
only suddenness can push things through
to be known at all—
that he was weeping
in his labours at her; she sensed

more than felt the tears
fall through both their sweats
and bead up their salt, their sand,
inside her rednesses:
she had to walk.
she knew then that she had to walk
great distances.

the family had come from ireland,
evolved its twilled thread of generations
into a design, like the design
we'd see in nerves.
and, in pacing back through that
progress, she found a whole
world-behind-the-mirror
of duplicates and equivalents
—small caches of foreign cousins,
removed twice and living in towns
or on stone-rut farms—
all repeatable milk-faces that,
like their american matches,
blemished too easily; aged too quick.
it all seemed like an album
read backwards—a chinese history—
the point of it found not in its pinnacle
but in its founding,
in the incepted seed
that was and always had been
the full-blown tree.
in many ways it was a grim and verdant
landscape, the medieval green
half taken from the sea encroaching;
half, she said, drawn out of some
forty shades of mould.
too wet, the sky hung as heavy as earth;
the land as porous as the air.
the heart hung: a cupboard left open.
all she saw was heavy with itself.
she walked north-west
across grassland, stone,
until, at last, the fog and sea-breath,
the tight, wet hills sliding down
with periwinkle

became a feeling—the national feeling,
she insisted—and a simple one: a fear
of the flesh, of the lung—the terrible
sense that any heart that beat
was a heart black with lust, with loss,
and one better off not beating at all;
the sense that the only peace
one ever saw, hovering over this damp earth,
came when one saw a piece of poor flesh
surrender, dry, and die.
she wondered with the arrival at every town
what had come down the genes
and across the sea to her: what she'd
inherited through marriage.
at limerick, she arrived in the midst
of a wake—a dim uncle, a tall man,
thin like herself, who had always worn
gray—a great story-teller, they told her;
they told her his story.
they also showed her his corpse.
it wore a heavy suit, as his body
seldom had.
there were photographs in the coffin
of him as a boy; aunts who'd
heard of her grief at home were
pointedly kind—they patted her,
sharing her sorrow like
a milky cup of tea.
they brought the widow to her.
she pressed her grieving fist of beads
into her hands: "commit yourself
to circumstance," the woman told her;
there was great bitterness in her,
"you're not a girl anymore, you know."

after this she stayed at inns,
avoiding the relatives. at night,
she read maps; drank stout alone in pubs.
soon she found she chose to walk
at night; it involved her less
and it was without great difficulty.
she had good vision in the dark.
she rarely fell. and when she did

she nearly enjoyed the abrupt break
in her pace,
the momentary drop into a shallow well
of sweetfern—she fell as a child falls
from its own history. in the dark,
she saw and longed for no aunt,
only for wood, the surrender to water,
dark earth, to the dog in the distance
confused by sheep. the many
blind grasses were as kind as hair.
the many invisible mosses gracious
on their mounds of new rock:
asleep or awake
she thought continually of his body
in the chair.
at sligo
the hiking grew arduous; with double the
effort, she threw herself at it;
made a discipline of it, a game of counts.
it became her—or became whatever
part of her that needed a body walking
in sweat to surface itself.
relieved, she vacated herself.
the walking legs still missed him:
the back felt relieved at being away.
the cheek worried; the foot fled the worryings
again and again, until the body,
taken altogether as a single-purposed
engine, made a green blur of concern
—a blur also of love and longing, of
the entrapment and the four winds that
passed outside their window at home.
she put miles underfoot eroding the hollow
lightness of his chair, his useless sweat,
the maddening, calling smell of it,
the past, once clearly theirs, now
embedded like a metal van in a wall
off in the delimited future—yes to make
a blur of that finality, that endurance,
and of the moonlight, the streetlight,
the daylight, the dark
laying down its smooth and gradual weight
upon his motherish chest,

his shoulders, of his thick throat
and yes! the dead, large man-sac!
the dragging flag of flesh down there
between unspeaking, deaf legs! yes!
a blur of that, god yes! of that and of
the anger, yes and of the hated life
and the love of him! of his pains
and cutting down, of the loss of all and
any meaning in the day, of impossible
necessity! of daily prevention!
yes a blur of all of it—a miasma, god,
that erased that world where only
the cool chair existed
amid the swing of chromium rings
and impossible love.

at errigal, at dawn, she slept:
she dreamed: it was night at home.
the mercury light fell from the streetpole,
the chalk light from the moon.
he sat nude in the chair.
it was oppressively hot.
he was sweating in the dim light.
the aluminum poles, the tacky plastic
pad were wet with it.
the metal chilled the skin of his arm,
his back. she felt the odd blunted
sense of it cooling obliquely
against the back of his thighs,
his legs: the lame sac, the penis
spread out flat on the seat.
it was a feeling like being half
in water.
she was calm in the dream, in errigal,
the mother of feelings, all in order,
in equipoise.
she reviewed his body, his muscled face;
she knew the man inside.
his thighs were like stone.
the absence in his legs was an aching
in hers.
she felt the vast fever burn behind his eyes—
and knew in the most amazing way

that nothing had changed—nothing: that
this was their life, unadorned,
seated in a dream. at once
she felt a great feeling in her;
told herself that she must remember
to straddle his shoulders
when next they met, to trust the centre
of her hips to his mouth,
to cradle his big head with her knees
and, while the rings turned silent
in every direction from their ropes,
to give to his teeth
a string of pearls from out of her womb,
while whispering yes yes
oh lover yes.

Wrestling with Angels

All night, hip out of joint,
he grips the cool muscles
of the stranger, throws him twice

but can't pin him to the earth:
shoulder blades flex like wings
and spring him loose. He is not even

breathing hard. Jacob knows.
Hobbling, he plants his good heel
for leverage. Their footprints

in the dirt scrape out the six points
of a star. Lunging, he clutches
the man and they spiral, locked

like dancers. Jacob
shuts his eyes tight, tight,
and holds on.

At dawn the blessing comes: watch him,
breathless, pull his new name Israel
over his head like a robe.

Reprinted from *The Keeper of Juno's Swans*, edited by J. R. LeMaster; copyright © 1979 by Baylor University Press.

After Being Paralyzed from the Neck Down for Twenty Years, Mr. Wallace Gets a Chin-Operated Motorized Wheelchair

For the first time in twenty years
he is mobile, roaring through corridors,
bouncing off walls, out of control,
breaking doorways, tables, chairs,
and regulations. The hallways stretch out
behind him, startled, amazed,
their plaster and wallpaper gaping,
while somewhere far off,
arms spastically flailing,
the small nurses continue to call:
Mr. Wallace . . . Mr. Wallace . . .

Eventually he'll listen to reason
and go quietly back to his room,
docile, repentant, and sheepish, promising
not to disappoint them again.
The day shift will sigh and go home.
But, in the evening, between feeding and bedtime,
when they've finally left him alone,
he'll roar over to the corner
and crash through the window
stopping only to watch
the last geese rising,
rising by the light of the snow.

Reprinted from *Plums, Stones, Kisses & Hooks* by Ronald Wallace by permission of the University of Missouri Press; copyright © 1981 by Ronald Wallace.

Recovery Song

I've put the deathbed frown behind me
the frame that languors in the night.
I've left the shadows begging at the door—
I'm a flyer now
a full pound lighter.

I glide downtown
to the family chambers:
my father, listening now
meeting me eye to eye
and music all through the rooms.

I've put off gloom
the gleaming kind
that leaves the heart lost
high and dreaming—

Stumpfoot on 42nd Street

A Negro sprouts from the pavement like an asparagus.
One hand beats a drum and cymbal;
He plays a trumpet with the other.

He flies the American flag;
When he goes walking, from stump to stump,
It twitches, and swoops, and flaps.

Also, he has a tin cup which he rattles;
He shoves it right in your face.
These freaks are alive in earnest.

He is not embarrassed.
It is for you to feel embarrassed,
Or God, or the way things are.

Therefore he plays the trumpet
And therefore he beats the drum.

2

I can see myself in Venezuela,
With flowers, and clouds in the distance.
The mind tends to drift.

But Stumpfoot stands near a window
Advertising cameras, trusses, household utensils.
The billboards twinkle. The time
Is 12:26.

O why don't angels speak in the infinite
To each other? Why this confusion,
These particular bodies—
Eros with clenched fists, sobbing and cursing?

The time is 12:26.
The streets lead on in burning lines
And giants tremble in electric chains.

3

I can see myself in the middle of Venezuela
Stepping in a nest of ants.
I can see myself being eaten by ants.

My ribs are caught in a thorn bush
And thought has no reality.
But he has furnished his room

With a chair and table.
A chair is like a dog, it waits for man.
He unstraps his apparatus,

And now he is taking off his boots.
He is easing his stumps,
And now he is lighting a cigar.

It seems that a man exists
Only to say, Here I am in person.

9:00 A.M. at Broadway and Walnut on Your Birthday

FOR DICK

Hand in hand they start across.
One misshapen face paired with a second,
two followed by two more, their faults of birth
entrusted to each other. Some further kindness
taught them to count on my training. Not for
the body wrench that gets them going, the hard
learned shuffle. I stop for the light.
Easy with automatic.

The first two reach the curb, heads swung
to the bus, aged girl, doddering boy.
They have a place to go. From curb to curb
the brave retarded, 2, 4, 6, 8 resolute
in someone's love. I like that look.
Your love has made me brave.

Their skewed faces show no pain
at my applause—tears flung through
a glaring windshield. That bus
will take them where they're wanted.
They know when they're cheered.
I know the bearing of infirmity, resolve
that brakes on through a green light,
your grip tight on a birthright of compassion.
You'd say welcome if I brought them home.

Reprinted by permission of the author from *Mapping My Father* (Dooryard Press, 1981); copyright © by Ripley Schemm.

Bleeder

The bld. in my body weighs
7 lbs. for every 100 lbs. of me;
I weigh 150;
I own 10 lbs. of blood;
6 bbls. of bld. pass through my heart
every 2 or 3 mins.;
my heart manages enough work in 1 hr.
to lift a 160 lb. man 70 ft. into the air;

my bld. keeps me 98.6;
whole bld. can be kept for only 21 days;
I'm 9/10 water,
and men own more bld. cells than women,
than women own, I mean.
Look, I've written a kind of sonnet.

So I write.
So, I'm a *Hee moh* Fill *ih ack.*
I want you to recognize what I can do.
I don't mean to be hung up on numbs. and abbrvs.

I don't try to swim the lake or play football
or climb even small mountains;
possibly I'm frightened
of the mouths of scratching women;

but I debate and sing and paint;
I read a lot; I meditate;
I dream of unimaginable encounters;
I write a sports clmn. for my town paper.
Blood from animals with backbones differs
from the blood of insects and sponges.

You don't have to blame your mother, for God's sake;
after a while you don't blame your mother,
even if only men boast hemophilia.
It's the disease of kings, for God's sake;

Reprinted with permission from *Occupant Please Forward* by Hollis Summers; copyright © 1976 by Rutgers University, the State University of New Jersey.

your mother passes it along to you
accordings to laws.
Mendel's law is as much a law as anybody's law.
A woman has to give bleeding to 2/3 of her sons,
and 2/3 of her daughters give again;
everybody's mother hands him something or other
he doesn't know what to do with;
so does everybody's father.

I would not like to make anything of being
an only child collecting all the thirds.

Factor VIII, that's the secret,
Like frozen orange juice, in a refrigerator;
In 10 min. you can inject yourself.

In the old days you had to spend 3 days
in a hospital every time you bled;
If you took a trip, you made your route
Where hospitals hovered.

I own a portable refrigerator.
In the old days you blamed your mother.
Factor VIII,
There's nothing mystic about it:
It's not Factor VII,
For God's sake.

Gauze over a wound acts as a network.
Clots form.
Anybody's bruise means
Bleeding inside.
We use a lot of gauze in the theater.
Almost everybody uses gauze,
Hiding behind laws and factors.

I'm headed for a camping trip now
directing a bunch of kids who bleed;
I'll argue with them and direct them in a play;
we'll sing and take walks,
surrounding a portable refrigerator.
Everybody's an artist and an accident,
for God's sake.

Waiting for Happy

A traveling preacher came through our town last summer and held a re-
vival that went on for four days, and while I remember many things that
that preacher said, one in particular sticks in my mind. He said that each
of us is special in the eyes of God. Just as every child is special in the eyes
of a parent, no matter how many kids that parent has, so each one of us is
special in the sight of God, no matter how unimportant our lives may
seem. To God we are all as important as President Carter himself, because
we're all God's children, even if we only live in a little town like our town
and work at a job the way I do over at the ball bearing plant in Edgewood.
Now it's a year later and as we young men gather in front of what used to
be Happy's barber shop to talk and smoke and pass a bottle of sweet wine
back and forth, I wonder about what that preacher said. There's Kendall
Misemer, for instance, who wanted to be a lawyer and settled for working
in his cousin's feed store, and I can't see anything special about him, but
maybe God can. And there's Mike Norris, who bought a motorcycle on
his sixteenth birthday, smashed it up real bad the very next day, and has
never done anything since then except sit around his mother's house
soaking up television. And sometimes I think I see something wistful in
the faces of my friends, something like when we were all kids together
and still had hopes and dreams, and I wonder if they see that in me, too.
Well, maybe the preacher was right and maybe he was wrong, but there
was something special about Happy Pankiewicz, and I want to tell you
about him, because sometimes I think the reason we sit around outside
that old barber shop is that we wish Happy would come back. Yes, we're
all waiting for Happy, just the way we did when we were boys and he used
to come peddling down Main Street on his ice cream bike. Yes, Happy
was special, and he was special not only in the eyes of God but in the eyes
of men, right out front in plain sight, where you could see it. And sometimes I think that's what really counts, though I don't mean to blaspheme.

The first thing that made Happy special (well, *different* anyway) was
that he had only one arm. Now some men have only one arm because
they've been in a tractor accident and others have had an arm shot off in a
war, but Happy's case was different, because Happy was born without
his. Of course that story wasn't exciting enough for us when we were
kids, so we made up another one. We used to tell the real little kids that
Happy kept his arm in the freezer compartment of his ice cream bike, and
they believed us. One of them tried to climb in there to see it once when
Happy's back was turned. The kid upset the bike and sent popsicles and

fudgsicles spinning across the sidewalk. I wish I could tell you that Happy reacted to this like a jolly, good-hearted guy who loved kids, but I can't. No, Happy was furious. He caught that kid and fanned his bottom good, flailing away with his right arm, that is, his only arm, the one God gave him. He was very effective with what he had and that's what God expects from us—that is, to make the most of what he gave us.

Some men seem to have been born to peddle ice cream bikes in small towns. They love to see the expectant looks on people's faces when they hear the jingling of the bells and see that white wagon coming closer. But Happy wasn't one of those men. No, he hated it—hated the peddling, hated dipping his one hand in that freezer compartment, hated making change. One night the ice cream plant burned to the ground, and everyone was sad about that because it meant no more ice cream. But Happy wasn't sad. He spent a whole week celebrating, drinking up his final paycheck in the Muny Tavern, as delighted as a catfish on the bottom of the river when a barge dumps its garbage. Another thing that made Happy different was that he was independent. When other people were sad, he was happy, and when other people were happy, he acted sad. That's just the way he was.

Happy had ambitions like most men, but his were higher than most, which is another thing that made him different. One day he decided that he wanted to be a champion blue-grass fiddler, so he told everyone in town that this was his ambition. Everyone was kind of embarrassed and looked the other way, which made Happy mad. He sent away to Sears-Roebuck in Chicago for a fiddle, but when it came it was a cornet, and finally he just said, "There just ain't no way I'm gonna learn to fiddle on this thing," so he gave it up. For a while he did the calling at the barn dances on Saturday nights at the high school gym and that seemed to satisfy him. But then people stopped coming to the dances because they preferred to stay home and watch television. The way they reasoned it, why should they get all sweaty and tired in that high school gym when they could stay home and sit in a comfortable chair and watch "Lawrence Welk" and "Hee-Haw!" So they stopped having the dances.

There were lots of things Happy could do with one arm that many men in our town couldn't do with two, and one of these was to pass the basket on the long pole during the offertory at Mass in the Catholic church. Happy could do this because he was a deacon in the church and as a deacon he had the power to decide who would pass the basket, and he always decided on himself. The men with two arms weren't deacons, so they had to stand around saying, "Go, Happy, go!" and "You show 'em, Happy!" under their breaths. Happy always dropped the basket two or three times during the ceremony, but no one dared say anything. A lot of people were afraid of Happy. I remember those coins rolling down the aisle after Happy dropped the basket. But any kid who went after them got slapped by his mother. Now it's instinct in a kid to dart after rolling coins, but we learned self-control, and if I trace it back I find I owe that trait in me to Happy and his basket on a long pole in the Catholic church so long ago.

After Happy gave up on the idea of being a fiddler, he decided he wanted to be a brain surgeon, and he told everybody about that. It was a topic of conversation for about six months in our town, and some people laughed and others were concerned that Happy had gone "mental" and would have to be put away. But finally Fatso Collins drew Happy aside and said, "Look, Happy, why don't you become the town barber? You'll be working with heads just like a brain surgeon, and it won't take near as much study." Our other barber had drowned himself in a water tank after his dog died, so we were without a barber. Happy had never been much for studying, as Fatso knew. "No studying at all," he went on. "All you have to do is practice for a while with a bowl and some scissors on an Angora cat or a Pekinese dog or a goat, and when you learn to trim it nice and even, well, you're in business!"

So Happy became the barber in our town, and that was something special because he was probably the only one-armed barber in the state— or maybe in the nation or even in the whole world for all we knew. We were proud because our town had something no other town had, a one-armed barber. We used to go down to the shop to watch him sweep the hair out, holding the broom under his chin and sweeping away hell-bent-for-leather with his one arm. It was a glorious sight for a kid to see and I loved it. But then the price of haircuts went up from a quarter to half a dollar to ninety cents, and the popcorn processing plant closed down for good throwing men out of work, and wives began to cut the hair of their men and kids at home, so Happy lost out in the end. People would walk by and see Happy sitting in his shop with nothing to do, staring into space and looking glum. That was sad. Pretty soon the shop was only open three times a week. Then that become once a week (Saturday). And then it closed down for good. Then Happy became the bartender at the Muny Tavern, for though people will give up going to a barber shop they will never give up going to the bar. No matter how broke they are, it seems they just have to be with friends and drink, and the Muny Tavern was just about the only place in our town where you could do this.

At first Jim Folsom, who owned the place, was scared to hire Happy because Happy had a history of alcoholism and when he was on one of his binges he was a frightening sight to behold, with his violent Polish temper, which he had inherited from his father. But Happy signed the pledge and gave it to Jim and said, "I want you to paste that up right over the bar there where everybody can see it. It's my promise that I will not drink one drop of liquor while I am in your employ, so help me God!" So he was hired. But it's just human nature that as soon as this got around town every man had to test it out. They were all dead set on being the instruments of Happy's downfall. They'd crowd into that bar when he was working and say, "Have a drink on me, Happy!" and "Drinks for everybody, including the bartender!" But Happy never touched a drop. Sometimes glasses would be lined up all along the bar like sets of tin soldiers, but they were all untouched by Happy. Then Jim and Happy thought they'd play a joke on the town. They took an empty whiskey bottle, filled it with tea and put it under the bar. Then Happy told everyone, "To hell with my pledge. Saturday night I'm going to outdrink every man in this town. And if you men can come up with two hundred dollars, I'll match you the same amount, just to show you I can do it." So every man in town came in that Saturday night, many of them bringing their wives with them, and Happy matched every man drink for drink and he never got drunk. Of course he was drinking the tea. Every man except Happy fell down drunk on the floor that fateful night. Happy just stood there, pouring out drinks for them, and every once in a while winking at Jim Folsom. Happy took the two hundred dollars too, but later it came out about the tea because Jim let it slip, and Happy had to give it all back, which was only fair. Jim said, "Happy has a job in this here bar for life!" And he talked about making him a partner in the business, which was about the only profitable one in our town.

But then, one night while Happy was tending bar, a man walked in, pulled a gun and said, "Give me all the money in that cash register over there!" Happy did as the man told him. It only came to about thirty dollars, and by giving it to him Happy probably saved his own life and the lives of every man in that bar. But later Happy heard someone say, "Why didn't Happy put up a fight? I always figured Happy for more of a man than that." This hurt his pride and it preyed on his mind so much that after a while he told Jim, "I can't stand it no more," and he quit. And that was the end of that.

Happy fell in love, as all men do at least once in their lives, and, as happens to all men too, he broke his heart over it. The woman called herself Dolores, but some men said they'd known her as "Rose" when she worked for Big Emma at her whorehouse in Bremerton. Of course no one ever told Happy about this. Dolores worked as a waitress in the Midway Truck Stop for a while, but after she started going with Happy she quit out there. He made her do it because he didn't like truckers looking at his woman. Now the thing about Dolores was, she had a glass eye. No one knew how she came to lose her real one, but she had replaced it with one made of glass. One day, when Happy and Dolores were fishing from a boat on the Blue Bruise River (which is the name of the river that runs past our town), the eye fell out, dropped into the water, and passed out of sight. The very next day Dolores left town with her friend Rita LaMars and neither of them was ever heard from again, though it seems to me now that someone said they went to New Mexico or Arizona or somewhere like that to get jobs in the aircraft industry. Anyway, losing Dolores broke Happy's heart, and one day, fishing in the same spot on the river, he caught a fish, split it open to clean it and—why, there was that glass eye right there in the intestine, looking like a kid's marble in the middle of a dish of noodles. Happy broke down and cried. He cried all the way home from the river, and then he cried in his house, and after that (because crying by himself got monotonous) he went out and cried all over town. He cried at the gas station, at the feed store, at the supermarket, and at Helen's Cafe out near the highway. At night people heard him crying at the water tower, which was the place he used to go with his love to do what lovers do. He cried for days. There was just no end to it. Folks talked about bringing in a doctor from out of town and a teacher said that Happy needed a psychiatrist . . . Then, early one morning, someone saw Happy on the edge of town, hitchhiking, his one arm extended and his thumb out. A truck stopped, picked him up and he was on his way. He waved once and gave our town the finger, and that was the last anybody ever saw of Happy Pankiewicz.

Now on summer nights we sit on the rotting steps of Happy's barber shop, slapping at mosquitoes and passing a bottle of Annie Greenspring wine back and forth, and sometimes someone will say, "Gee! Think Happy will ever come back? Ridin' down Main Street the way he used to on his ice cream bike? Gosh, that Happy, he was special. He really was." But last week I guess I had too much wine, and I was feeling blue about being laid off at the plant, so I said, "It's not so! Happy wasn't special! He was just a God damned bore like everyone else in this town!" And then, in the shocked silence that followed, I don't know why but—well, I just broke down and cried.

Saint Flannery

"She could never be a saint, but she thought she could be a martyr if they killed her quick."

F. O'C.

At Lourdes everybody drank from the cup
passed round. She put her metal crutches down
and counted those ahead—about forty.
In Rome she sat eager on the front row
and the Pope gave her a special blessing
"on acct. the crutches." She felt herself
a twelve year old, "a very ancient twelve,"
yet watched him as she would her characters.
He had "the special super-aliveness
that holiness is." She'd seen it in swans,
peacocks, Muscovy ducks and Chinese geese.
Now she who said she'd see us all in hell
before she made her first graceful move must
accept these candles brought on knees to her.

Reprinted by permission of the author from *The Touched Life* (Scarecrow Press, 1982); copyright © by David Ray.

Pizarro Teaches the Mentally Retarded to Swim

And when it's over, go with the child
to the dressing hut. Make sure he takes
his friend's washcloth with him. If someone
is there to help him you need not stay
but if no one in the hut is able to help
then dress him. Then take him to the person
in charge of transportation.

After, I drag in the heat. All around
there are fine trees. This is a willow
and that is a beech. I go upstream
the way I did years ago, when the jailer's
niece ran away with me. She carried the
local beer.

We laughed when fish spat bubbles
in the loud butter of the frying pan,
we said those fish were not our ancestors.
We fooled in the blackberries and dreamed
up a fine story: the stains on our hands
were false, and different from the shadow
a face leaves on flesh.

I sit down in the water. The animal screams
of delight are gone, the kid who learned
to dive is gone. The girl who asked the
kitty in the water is home asleep. Turtles
are back to normal.

I put my ears underwater, to wash out
years of wandering. I hear a song from frogs,
about how they want children to pick them up.
And I see a stable fire walking down the road
to church. No one home, the lord went swimming.

To One Deaf

Already you are
in the new country
listening to silence
which flows like a river
from the eyes of the Alone.

Sound cannot trespass
your kingdom where you live
with the word who makes clean
the words of men.

In your country
the sun does not set
and from you mouth
lilies spring like alleluias.

Who will say you do not hear?
Not one who has listened
to an unrung bell.